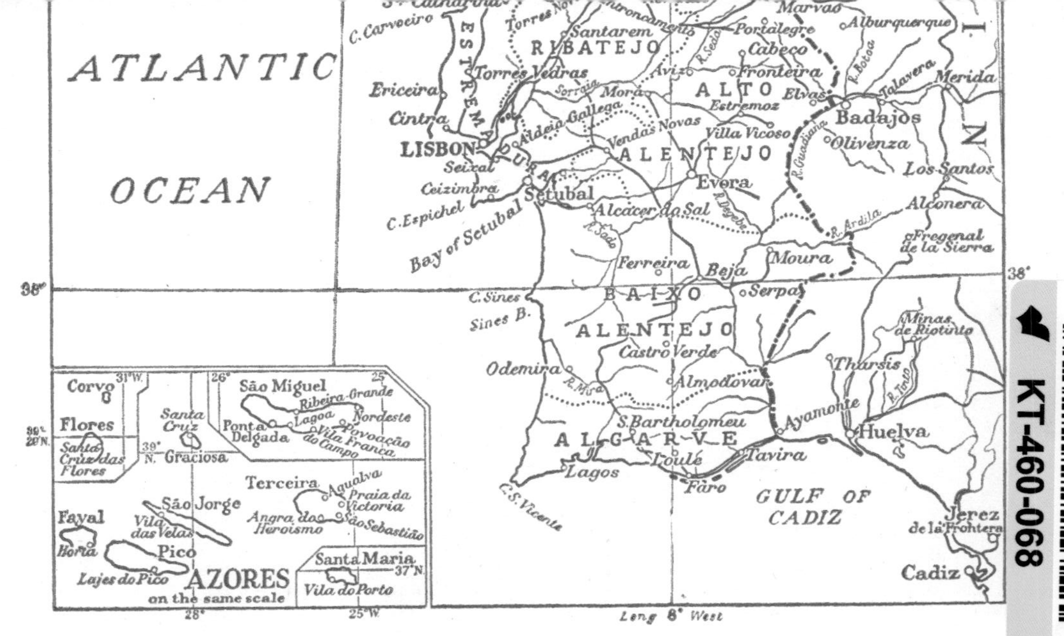
ATLANTIC
OCEAN
C. Carvoeiro
Torres Novas
Santarem
RIBATEJO
ESTREMADURA
Torres Vedras
Ericeira
Cintra
LISBON
Seixal
Ceizimbra
C. Espichel
Bay of Setubal
Setubal
Aldeia Gallega
Sorraia
Mora
Aviz
R. Seda
Portalegre
Marvao
Alburquerque
Cabeco
Fronteira
ALTO
Elvas
Estremoz
Vendas Novas
Villa Vicoso
ALENTEJO
Evora
R. Degebe
Alcacer da Sal
R. Sado
Ferreira
Beja
Moura
Serpa
Badajos
Olivenza
R. Guadiana
R. Botoa
Talavera
Merida
Los Santos
Alconera
R. Ardila
Fregenal de la Sierra
38°
C. Sines
Sines B.
BAIXO
ALENTEJO
Castro Verde
Odemira
R. Mira
Almodovar
S. Bartholomeu
ALGARVE
Loulé
Lagos
Faro
Tavira
C. S. Vicente
Ayamonte
Tharsis
Minas de Riotinto
R. Tinto
Huelva
GULF OF CADIZ
Jerez de la Frontera
Cadiz
Long 8° West
Corvo
31°W.
Flores
Santa Cruz das Flores
Santa Cruz
39° N.
Graciosa
39° 20' N.
26°
25°
São Miguel
Ribeira Grande
Nordeste
Ponta Delgada
Lagoa
Povoação
Vila Franca do Campo
Terceira
Agualva
Praia da Victoria
Angra do Heroismo
São Sebastião
São Jorge
Vila das Velas
Fayal
Horta
Pico
Lajes do Pico
Santa Maria
37°N.
Vila do Porto
AZORES
on the same scale
28°
25°W.

COLLINS
PHRASE BOOKS

Collins Phrase Books

ITALIAN · SPANISH · RUSSIAN
FRENCH · PORTUGUESE · GERMAN

INSTANT

A complete Index, practical subdivision of subject and bold, clear type ensure speed of reference.

EASY

Clear and accurate pronunciation of every phrase is rendered by English syllables.

MODERN

Up-to-date material deals fully with Air Travel, Motoring, Visa Requirements, etc.

ACCURATE

Expert advice has been taken to ensure idioms and general information are current and correct.

PRACTICAL

The choice of useful phrases and sentences and general advice are invaluable to tourist and business man.

COLLINS
PHRASE BOOKS

PORTUGUESE

Edited by

N. J. LAMB, M.A.

Lecturer in Portuguese in the University of Liverpool

COLLINS
LONDON AND GLASGOW

GENERAL EDITOR: J. B. FOREMAN M.A.
First published, 1958
Reprinted, 1964

PRINTED IN GREAT BRITAIN
BY COLLINS CLEAR-TYPE PRESS

CONTENTS

ÍNDICE DE MATÉRIAS

INTRODUCTION

INFORMATION.—This can be obtained from the Casa de Portugal, 20 Lower Regent Street, London, S.W.1. In Lisbon the tourist can get information from the S.N.I. (Secretariado Nacional da Informação), Praça dos Restauradores. There is a branch of the S.N.I. in the Praça Dom João I in Oporto. Estoril has a Junta de Turismo in the Arcadas do Parque. There is a tourist information office at the railway station in Sintra, and Funchal has a similar office in the Avenida Arriaga. There are municipal information offices in the larger towns.

PRELIMINARY REQUIREMENTS.—Citizens of the United Kingdom and the Republic of Ireland do not require a visa for entering Portugal, provided their stay does not exceed 60 days. Valid passports are, however, essential. The addresses of some Portuguese Consulates are:

103 Sloan Street, London, S.W.1.
1 Falkner Square, Liverpool, 8.
59 Queen Street, Cardiff.
200 St. Vincent Street, Glasgow, C.2.

ROUTES TO PORTUGAL.—The usual route by rail is via London–Paris–Hendaye–Irun–Salamanca–Vilar Formoso –Lisbon. The "Sud-Express" is the most comfortable and rapid train but also, of course, the most expensive. Time-tables and costs can be checked at the travel agencies. The sea voyage to Lisbon, which often affords the opportunity of spending some hours ashore at Corunna, Vigo or Leixões (for Oporto) takes about three days. The usual sailings are from Southampton, Liverpool and London. The offices of most of the shipping companies are near the Cais do Sodré station in Lisbon. B.E.A. and T.A.P. (Transportes Aéreos Portugueses) have regular flights to Lisbon.

Currency.—Travellers from the United Kingdom must comply with British regulations concerning the foreign currency allowance. Travellers' cheques are cashed without difficulty in Portugal on presentation of the passport; the banks there require the traveller's address in Portugal.

The unit of currency is the "escudo", and the rate of exchange in 1958 is approximately 80 escudos to the £. For practical purposes, one escudo may be taken as equivalent to 3*d.* There are 100 "centavos" in one escudo. A "conto" is 1,000 escudos.

Prices are written thus:

5 $ 40 (i.e. 5 escudos, 40 centavos);
0 $ 80 (i.e. 80 centavos).

Transport.—Information at the travel agencies and the railway stations. Expresses are known as "Rápidos"; the "Comboio-Correio" is a stopping-train; "Automotoras" are Diesel trains. There is a frequent ferry service for passengers and cars from Lisbon across the Tagus. Lisbon and Oporto have good tram and bus services at very reasonable prices, ranging from 50 centavos to 1 $ 50 in trams and 50 centavos to 3 $ 00 in buses. Taxis are numerous and fairly cheap.

Meals.—There is no rationing. Meals are generally good and abundant. Ordinary red or white table wine is served with luncheon and dinner. Service is very pleasant and obliging: the Portuguese take a genuine interest in the visitor's appetite and are always anxious to comply with his tastes and wishes, but you must not expect bacon and eggs! Breakfast, often served to the guest in his bedroom, consists of coffee (or tea, if asked for) with rolls and butter and, sometimes, jam. Luncheon is served as a rule between 12.30 and 2 p.m., dinner from 7.30 until about 9 p.m.; these times may vary, but dinner is rarely served as late as in Spain. Afternoon tea is not generally served unless specially requested; the tea is weak and perhaps not altogether satisfactory by British standards, but Portuguese cakes are good.

Port wine is by no means the only wine of high quality produced in Portugal: "Dão", "Colares", "Vinho verde", among many others, are deservedly popular.

The café is very popular in Portugal, as in Spain. A small cup or glass of coffee costs about one escudo, to which a tip of perhaps 50 centavos may be added.

Tipping.—In hotels and boarding-houses a service charge of 10% is added to the bill. But this need not exclude an extra tip if the tourist feels he has had good service from the employees. Taxi-drivers might receive 10 to 15% of the fare. Cloak-room tips vary from 1 $ 00 to 2 $ 50. Porters have fixed charges for carrying luggage, but a tip of perhaps 1 $ 00 to 2 $ 00 could be given. Shoe-blacks are given a small tip.

Amusements.—Cinemas show many British and American films. The sound-track is not usually "dubbed"; only the sub-titles are in Portuguese. Lisbon and Oporto have some night-clubs but many visitors make for the "Restaurantes Típicos" to hear the *fados* sung. Both the night-clubs and the "Restaurantes Típicos" are rather expensive. Bull-fighting, from May to October, is not nearly so prominent as in Spain, nor, incidentally, is the bull killed; football is much more popular. Facilities for tennis, golf, fishing, camping are available: information on these and on the regional fairs and festivals can be obtained from the tourist bureaux.

Motoring.—The British tourist can acquire information and the requisite documents from the Automobile Association or the Royal Automobile Club. In Portugal the principal office of the "Automóvel Clube de Portugal" is at 24 Rua Rosa Araújo, Lisbon, and the club has a branch in Oporto.

Petrol, which is not rationed, was 5 escudos per litre in 1957 (i.e. about 5*s.* a gallon), and oil 16 $ 50 per litre.

General.—Attention should be paid to regulations concerning dress on beaches and when entering churches. Bathing costume regulations are fairly strict, and scanty bathing costumes are prohibited. Men can now, however, bathe wearing trunks only; women must wear a complete swimsuit: bikinis and two-piece costumes are not permitted. On entering churches, women should cover their heads, arms and legs, and men should not enter in shorts.

Forms of address are complicated in Portugal. There is no simple translation of the English "you" which can be universally applied. The best plan is probably to avoid "you" altogether and use only the verb-form (as in the majority of the phrases in this book). A man of good social standing is addressed as "Vossa Excelência" (vos-esh-sĕ-le^{n}′-see-ă); "madam" is "minha senhora" (meen′-yă sĕn-yoh′-ră) or "Vossa Excelência" (both more widely used than "madam" in the United Kingdom). A maid in a hotel or boarding-house is addressed as "menina" (mĕ-nee′-nă). When speaking to porters, guides, etc., "o senhor" (oo sĕn-yohr′) can be used as a translation of the English "you".

On stopping somebody in order to inquire the way, one can preface one's inquiry with either "Fazia favor" (fă-zee′-ă fă-vohr′) or "Com licença" (ko^{n} lee-se^{n}′-să).

To call for attention in a café—though this is rarely necessary, since waiters are alert—one can say "faz favor" (fash fă-vohr′); in cafés, some Portuguese are adept at hissing (*psst!*) for attention, but this is perhaps undignified, and difficult for the outsider to do well! It is not customary to clap one's hands or call out "criado" (waiter).

There is an increasing number of Portuguese now speaking English, particularly in the larger towns. French is also widely known, and Spanish is readily understood.

PRONUNCIATION OF PORTUGUESE

THE pronunciation of Portuguese is undoubtedly difficult. The phonetic patterns of the language are much more complicated than those of Spanish. Hence, while a tourist knowing Spanish will have little difficulty in reading Portuguese and being understood when he speaks Spanish—or even when he attempts to speak Portuguese with a Spanish accent—he will find it far from easy to understand what is being said to him in reply.

No transcription into English symbols can represent with complete accuracy the complexities and nuances of Portuguese sounds, a full description of which is beyond the limits of this book. A single letter may have different sounds, depending on its position within the word and on its relation to other letters: thus, *o* has three values, *s* and *x* have four. The transcription scheme used here is intended to serve only as an approximation to the correct pronunciation.

Portuguese is spoken rapidly, with much slurring of unstressed syllables, linking together of words, and assimilation of sounds.

In this scheme the stress is to be placed on the syllable immediately preceding the acute accent mark (′).

Symbol employed	*Portuguese spelling*	*Symbol represents approximately the following English sounds*
ah	a	long open *a* as in f*a*ther, r*a*ther.
ar	ar	long open *a* plus trilled *r*, as in st*ar*ry.
a	a	a somewhat shorter, but still open, *a*; like Northern English l*a*d.
ă	a	close or "obscure" *a* as in *a*bove, *a*bout, sof*a*.
ăr	ar	close *a* plus trilled *r*; roughly as in sug*ar*y, summ*ar*y.

Symbol employed	*Portuguese spelling*	*Symbol represents approximately the following English sounds*
air	er	as in h*air*y, with trilled *r* always.
ay	e	as in st*ay*, pl*ay*, but without final glide.
ay-ee	ei	as in pl*ay*, plus a rapidly spoken *ee*; roughly equivalent to the sharp cry h*ey*!
e	e	as in b*e*t, g*e*m.
e-ee	éi	as in b*e*t, plus rapidly spoken *ee*.
e-oo	éu	as in b*e*t, plus rapidly spoken *oo*.
ĕ	e, i	close, "obscure" *e*, as in op*e*n, spok*e*n.
ĕr	er	close *e* as in op*e*n, plus trilled *r*; roughly as *er* in Ev*er*est, wat*er*y.
ee	i, e	as in m*ee*t, s*ee*n.
ish	es (when unstressed at beginning of word)	as in d*ish*.
o	o	open *o*, as in t*o*p.
oh	o, ou	close *o*; a pure vowel as in Northern English c*o*pe, m*o*st.
or	or	as *or*, but with trilled *r*, in f*or*, *or*gan.
oh-ee	oi	as Northern English m*o*st, plus rapidly spoken *ee*; roughly as *owy* in sh*owy*.

Symbol employed	*Portuguese spelling*	*Symbol represents approximately the following English sounds*
oo	o, u	as in m*oo*n.
ow	au	as in n*ow*.
oy	ói	as in b*oy*.
ȳ	ai	as in st*y*le.
b	b	as in English.
d	d	as in English, but rather softer when between two vowels (though not as soft as in Spanish).
f	f	as in English.
g	g (+consonant or a, o, u)	as in *g*o, *g*et.
k	c (+consonant or a, o, u); qu (+e, i)	as *k* in English.
ks	x	as *ks* in boo*ks*.
l	l	as in English.
ly, l-y	lh	as *li* in mil*li*on.
m	m	as in English.
n	n	as in English.
ny, n-y	nh	as *ny* in ca*ny*on.
p	p	as in English.
r	r, rr	a strongly trilled *r* as in Scots.
s	s, ss, x, ç, c (+e, i)	as *s* in *s*un, hou*s*e.
sh	s, ch, x, z	as in *sh*op.
t	t	as in English.
v	v	as in English.
w	u	as *w* in *w*in.
gw	go, gu (+a)	as *gw* in wi*gw*am.
kw	qu (+a)	as *kw* in boo*kw*orm.

Symbol employed	*Portuguese spelling*	*Symbol represents approximately the following English sounds*
mw	mu (+i)	as *mw* in tra*mw*ay.
y + vowel	i (+a, o, u, sometimes), and part of sounds of "nh" and "lh" + vowel)	as *y* in *y*ou.
z	s, z, x	as *z* in English.
zh	s, z, j, g (+e, i)	as *s* in mea*s*ure.

Note: Portuguese *h* is always silent. *E* at the end of a word of more than one syllable is usually silent but is often sounded when the following word begins with a vowel. *E* meaning "and" is always pronounced *ee*.

The nasalisation of vowels and diphthongs is a notable feature of Portuguese pronunciation, though the intensity of the nasalisation is weaker than in French. Nasalisation is shown here by ^{n} after a vowel or diphthong. Thus *ee*^{n} represents a nasalised *ee* (*ee* pronounced through the nose) and *ow*^{n} is the nasalised *ow* of English n*ow*.

Nasalisation is shown in Portuguese spelling either by inserting a "til" (˜) over a vowel or by an *m* at the end of a word or by *m* or *n* plus a consonant.

Strictly speaking, the symbols printed here as *a*^{n}, *o*^{n}, *e*^{n}, oy^{n} represent closed nasalised vowels or diphthongs and approximate, therefore, to *ă*^{n}, *oh*^{n}, *ay*^{n}, *oh-ee*^{n}. But for practical purposes the symbols as given in the text will suffice.

Brazilian Portuguese

THE Portuguese spoken in Brazil differs in some respects from that of Portugal, as American-English differs from our own.

Generally, Brazilian pronunciation seems slower, more measured, with less linking of words, and is perhaps clearer to the English ear than the pronunciation of Portugal. The unstressed vowels, rapidly slurred over in Portugal, are heard more clearly in Brazil. Final *e* is sounded more frequently (e.g. "cidade": see-dah′-dee), but sometimes palatalises the preceding consonant (e.g. "diferente": dee-fĕ-re^{n}tsh′). *S* at the end of a syllable often remains as a "hard" *s* or *z*, instead of sounding as sh or zh (e.g. país: pa-ees′; escrevo: is-kray′-voo; desde: dez′-dee).

In vocabulary also there are occasional differences. For example: bonde = tramcar; cardápio = menu; discar = to dial a number; parada = a bus stop; senhorita = young lady, Miss; terno = suit; trem = train.

The spelling used throughout this book is up-to-date in conformity with the *Acordo Luso-Brasileiro* of 1945.

Notes on Grammar

1. All nouns in Portuguese are regarded as either masculine or feminine. Nouns ending in *o* are almost always masculine; nouns ending in *a*, *ção* and *dade* are almost always feminine. Where this rule varies, or where the nouns end in some other letter, the appropriate definite or indefinite article is given to indicate the gender.

The definite article ("the") before masculine nouns is *o* (plural *os*), before feminine nouns *a* (plural *as*). The masculine indefinite article ("a, an") is *um*; the feminine indefinite article is *uma*. The plural-ending of nouns is *s*.

2. After "sou" (I am), "estou" (I am), "sinto-me" (I feel) an adjective ending in *o* changes this ending to *a* if the speaker is a woman. For example, "estou cansado" (I am tired) is the form used by a man; a woman would say "estou cansada". Similarly, "sinto-me enjoada" (I feel seasick) is the form used by a woman. Also, a woman

says "obrigada" (thank you) while a man says "obrigado", and "sou inglesa" (I am English) instead of the masculine "sou inglês".

I wish to express my thanks to Miss Matilde Carreira, Dr. António Duarte and, in particular, my colleague, Dr. Firmino de Deus Crespo, for valuable assistance, and to Miss A. White for careful preparation of the typescript.

N.J.L.

PHRASES IN COMMON USE

Yes, No. | Sim, não.
see^{n}, now^{n}.

Please, Thank you. | Faz favor, obrigado.
fash fă-vohr′, oh-bree-gah′-doo.

Excuse me (=I am sorry). | Desculpe; perdão.
dish-koolp′; pĕr-dow^{n}′.

Excuse me (=may I pass ?). | Com licença.
ko^{n} lee-se^{n}′-să.

How much ? | Quanto ?
kwa^{n}′-too.

Where is ? | Onde é ?
o^{n}′-dee e.

How far ? | A que distância ?
ă kĕ deesh-ta^{n}′-see-ă.

When ? | Quando ?
kwa^{n}′-doo.

Don't mention it; not at all. | De nada.
dĕ nah′-dă.

What do you say ? | Como ?
koh′-moo.

Good morning. | Bom dia.
bo^{n} dee′-ă.

Good afternoon. | Boa tarde.
boh′-ă tard.

Good evening; Good night. | Boa noite.
boh′-ă noh′-eet.

Good-bye. | Adeus.
ă-day′-oosh.

English	Portuguese	Pronunciation
Good-bye (but meeting again soon).	Até logo.	ă-te′ lo′-goo.
Au revoir.	Até à vista.	ă-te′ ah veesh′-tă.
Do you speak English?	Fala inglês?	fa′-lă ee^{n}-glaysh′.
I do not speak Portuguese.	Não falo português.	now^{n} fa′-loo poor-too-gaysh′.
I do not understand.	Não percebo.	now^{n} pĕr-say′-boo.
Would you please speak more slowly.	Fazia favor de falar mais devagar.	fă-zee′-ă fă-vohr′ dĕ fă-lar′ mȳzh dĕ-vă-gar′.
Write it down please.	Faz favor de escrevê-lo.	fash fă-vohr′ dish-krĕ-vay′-loo.
You do not understand me.	Não me compreende.	now^{n} mĕ ko^{n}-pree-e^{n}d′.
How do you say —— in Portuguese?	Como se diz...em português?	koh′-moo sĕ deesh...e^{n} poor-too-gaysh′.
What time is it?	Que horas são?	kee o′-răsh sow^{n}.
Is it time to go?	São horas de partir?	sow^{n} o′-răzh dĕ păr-teer′.
I must go.	Devo ir.	day′-voo eer.
It is late.	É tarde.	e tard.
It is early.	É cedo.	e say′-doo.
Am I interrupting you?	Estou a interromper?	ish-toh′ ă ee^{n}-tĕ-ro^{n}-payr′.

Are you ready?	Está pronto?
ish-ta′ pro^n′-too.	
As soon as possible.	O mais cedo possível.
oo mӯsh say′-doo poo-see′-vĕl.	
At the latest.	O mais tardar.
oo mӯsh tăr-dar′.	
Bring ——	Traga...
trah′-gă.	
Come here.	Venha cá.
ven′-yă ka.	
Come in.	Entre.
e^n′-trĕ.	
Don't do that.	Não faça isso.
now^n fah′-să ee′-soo.	
Don't forget.	Não se esqueça.
now^n see ish-ke′-să.	
Fast.	Depressa.
dĕ-pre′-să.	
Wait!	Espere!
ish-pair′.	
How long must I wait?	Quanto tempo devo esperar?
kwa^n′-too te^n′-poo day′-voo ish-pĕ-rar′.	
Will it be long?	Demora muito?
dĕ-mo′-ră mwee^n′-too.	
I am busy.	Estou ocupado.
ish-toh′ oo-koo-pah′-doo.	
I am in a hurry.	Estou com pressa.
ish-toh′ ko^n pre′-să.	
I am hot, cold.	Tenho calor, frio.
ten′-yoo kă-lohr′, free′-oo.	
I am hungry, thirsty.	Tenho fome, sede.
ten′-yoo fom, sayd.	
I am tired.	Estou cansado.
ish-toh′ ka^n-sah′-doo.	

English	Portuguese	Pronunciation
I am glad.	Estou contente.	ish-toh′ ko^n-te^{n}t′.
I am annoyed.	Estou aborrecido.	ish-toh′ ă-boo-rĕ-see′-doo.
I am very sorry.	Sinto muito.	see^n′-too mwee^n′-too.
I think so.	Julgo que sim.	zhool′-goo kĕ see^n.
I don't think so.	Julgo que não.	zhool′-goo kĕ now^n.
I know.	Já sei.	zha say′-ee.
I don't know.	Não sei	now^n say′-ee.
I understand.	Percebo.	pĕr-say′-boo.
I want.	Quero.	kair′-oo.
I don't want.	Não quero.	now^n kair′-oo.
I have lost.	Perdi.	pĕr-dee′.
I hope.	Espero.	ish-pair′-oo.
I insist.	Insisto.	ee^n-seesh′-too.
I promise you.	Prometo-lhe.	proo-may′-too lyĕ.
Is it not so?	Não é?	now^n e.
I will give you my address.	Dou-lhe a minha direcção.	doh′-lyĕ ă meen′-yă dee-re-sow^n′.

Let us go for a walk.	Vamos dar um passeio.
vă′-moozh dar oo^{n} pă-say′-yoo.	
Listen.	Ouça. (Oiça.)
oh′-să (oh′-ee-să).	
Look out.	Cuidado. (Atenção.)
kwee-dah′-doo (ă-te^{n}-sow^{n}′).	
More or less.	Mais ou menos.
mȳz oh may′-noosh.	
Not so fast.	Não tão depressa.
now^{n} tow^{n} dĕ-pre′-să.	
Open the door.	Abra a porta.
abr′-ah por′-tă.	
Shut the window.	Feche a janela.
fesh ă zhă-ne′-lă.	
Please can you tell me?	Pode dizer-me, se faz favor?
pod dee-zayr′-mĕ, sĕ fash fă-vohr′.	
Please repeat.	Faz favor de repetir.
fash fă-vohr′ dĕ rĕ-pĕ-teer′.	
Speak to him (her).	Fale com ele (ela).
fal ko^{n} ayl, e′-lă.	
Tell him to wait.	Diga-lhe que espere.
dee′-gă-lyĕ kish-pair′.	
Wait a minute.	Espere um momento.
ish-pair′ oo^{n} moo-me^{n}′-too.	
Wait for us.	Espere por nós.
ish-pair′ poor nosh.	
We are in a hurry.	Estamos com pressa.
ish-tă′-moosh ko^{n} pre′-să.	
We are very grateful.	Estamos muito agradecidos.
ish-tă′-moosh mwee^{n}′-too ă-gră-dĕ-see′-doosh.	
What?	O quê?
oo kay.	

What is it?	O que é?
oo kee e.	
What does that mean?	Que quer dizer isto?
kĕ kair dee-zayr′ eesh′-too.	
What have I to pay?	Quanto devo pagar?
kwa^{n}′-too day′-voo pă-gar′.	
What is that for?	Para que é isso?
pă′-ră kee e ee′-soo.	
What is that in English, Portuguese?	O que é isso em inglês, português?
oo kee e ee′-soo e^{n} ee^{n}-glaysh′, poor-too-gaysh′.	
What is the matter?	O que é que se passa?
oo kee e kĕ sĕ pa′-să.	
What is your name?	Como se chama? (Qual é o seu nome?)
koh′-moo sĕ shă′-mă. (kwal e oo say′-oo nohm).	
What is your address?	Qual é a sua direcção?
kwal e ă soo′-ă dee-re-sow^{n}′.	
Where?	Onde?
o^{n}d.	
Where to?	Para onde?
pă′-ră o^{n}d.	
Where are you going?	Para onde vai?
pă′-ră o^{n}d vȳ.	
Where do you live?	Onde mora?
o^{n}d mo′-ră.	
Who is it? Who is there?	Quem é?
ke^{n} e.	
Where can I wash my hands?	Onde posso lavar as mãos?
o^{n}d po′-soo lă-var′ ăzh mow^{n}sh.	
Where is the W.C.?	Onde é a casa de banho, o lavatório, a toilette?
o^{n}d′-ee e ă kah′-ză dĕ băn′-yoo, oo lă-vă-to′-ree-oo, ă twa-let′.	

Where is the Post Office? | Onde é o correio?
o^{n}′-dee e oo koo-ray′-yoo.

Where is the Police Station? | Onde é a Polícia?
o^{n}′-dee e ă poo-lee′-see-ă.

Where is the British Consulate? | Onde é o Consulado Britânico?
o^{n}′-dee e oo ko^{n}-soo-lah′-doo bree-tă′-nee-koo.

Why, why not? | Porquê, porque não?
poor-kay′, poor′-kĕ now^{n}.

Will you come with me? | Quer vir comigo?
kair veer koo-mee′-goo.

TELEPHONING

Numbers are pronounced individually, e.g. 57892 *should be read: cinco, sete, oito, nove, dois;* 50063: *cinco, zero, zero, seis, três;* 66741: *seis, seis, sete, quatro, um. Numerals are given at the end of this book, see page* 131.

I want to telephone. | Quero telefonar.
kair′-oo tĕ-lĕ-foo-nar′.

Telephone directory. | Lista dos telefones.
leesh′-tă doosh tĕ-lĕ-fonsh′ .

Hello! | Está? Está lá?
ish-tah′, ish-tah′ lah.

Who is speaking? | Quem fala?
ke^{n} fa′-lă.

This is —— | Daqui fala...
dă-kee′ fa′-lă...

Can I speak to ——? | Posso falar com...?
po′-soo fă-lar′ ko^{n}...

A telephone call. | Uma chamada.
oo′-mă shă-mah′-dă.

Telephone. Telephone box. | O telefone. A cabine telefónica.
oo tĕ-lĕ-fon′, ă kă-been′ tĕ-lĕ-fo′-nee-kă.

English	Portuguese	Pronunciation
Operator.	Telefonista.	tĕ-lĕ-foo-neesh′-tă.
Engaged	Está interrompido.	ish-ta′ ee^{n}-tĕ-ro^{n}-pee′-doo.
The line is out of order.	Avariada.	ă-vă-ree-ah′-dă.
You're through.	Está ligado.	ish-ta′ lee-gah′-doo.
What number?	Que número?	kĕ noo′-mĕ-roo.
You gave me the wrong number.	Enganou-se.	e^{n}-gă-nohs′.
I shall ring later.	Chamarei mais tarde.	shă-mă-ray′-ee mȳsh tard.
Ring me up.	Telefone-me.	tĕ-lĕ-fon′-mĕ.
Telegrams.	Telegramas.	tĕ-lĕ-gră′-măsh.
I want to send a telegram.	Quero mandar um telegrama.	kair′-oo ma^{n}-dar′ oo^{n} tĕ-lĕ-gră′-mă.
Trunk call.	Chamada para troncas.	shă-mah′-dă pă′-ră tro^{n}-kăsh.
To dial (a number).	Marcar (um número).	măr-kar′ (oo^{n} noo′-mĕ-roo).

TRAVELLING

ARRIVING

When do we arrive at the frontier?	Quando chegamos à fronteira?
kwa^{n}′-doo shĕ-gă′-mooz ah fro^{n}-tay′-ee-ră.	
What station is this?	Que estação é esta?
kee ish-tă-sow^{n}′ e esh′-tă.	
How long does the train stop?	Quanto tempo pára o comboio?
kwa^{n}′-too te^{n}′-poo pah′-ră oo ko^{n}-boy′-yoo.	
Can I get out?	Posso descer?
po′-soo dĕsh-sayr′.	
How long does it take?	Quanto tempo leva?
kwa^{n}′-too te^{n}′-poo le′-vă.	
Can I break the journey?	Posso interromper a viagem?
po′-soo ee^{n}-tĕ-ro^{n}-payr′ ă vee-ah′-zhe^{n}.	
Have I time to go to the refreshment room?	Tenho tempo para ir ao bufete?
ten′-yoo te^{n}′-poo pă′-ră eer ow boo-fet′.	
Where is the refreshment room?	Onde é o bufete?
o^{n}′-dee e oo boo-fet′.	
Two cups of coffee.	Dois cafés.
doh′-eesh kă-fesh′.	
Is the train late?	O comboio vem atrasado?
oo ko^{n}-boy′-yoo ve^{n} ă-tră-zah′-doo.	
Tickets.	Os bilhetes.
oozh beel-yetsh′.	
I want a taxi.	Quero um táxi.
kair′-oo oo^{n} tak′-see.	

Where are the taxis? | Onde estão os táxis?
o^{n}d ish-tow^{n}′ oosh tak′-seesh.

Is it far to —— ? | É muito longe daqui a . . . ?
e mwee^{n}′-too lo^{n}zh dă-kee′ ă . . .

CHANGING TRAINS

Must I change trains? | Devo mudar?
day′-voo moo-dar′.

Where must I change? | Onde devo mudar?
o^{n}d day′-voo moo-dar′.

Is there a good connection? | Há uma boa ligação?
ah oo′-mă boh′-ă lee-gă-sow^{n}′.

From the same station? | Da mesma estação?
dă mezh′-mă ish-tă-sow^{n}′.

How long have I to wait? | Quanto tempo tenho de esperar?
kwa^{n}′-too te^{n}′-poo ten′-yoo dish-pĕ-rar′.

Is there a through train to ——? | Há um comboio directo para . . . ?
ah oo^{n} ko^{n}-boy′-yoo dee-re′-too pă′-ră . . .

Does the train go to ——? | O comboio vai para . . . ?
oo ko^{n}-boy′-yoo vȳ pă′-ră . . .

Does the train pass through ——? | O comboio passa por . . . ?
oo kon-boy′-yoo pa′-să poor . . .

Does it stop at ——? | Pára em . . . ?
pah′-ră e^{n} . . .

Is there a dining-car? | Há um vagão-restaurante?
ah oo^{n} vă-gow^{n}′ rĕsh-tow-ra^{n}t′.

Is the train for —— in? | O comboio para . . . chegou?
oo ko^{n}-boy′-yoo pă′-ră . . . shĕ-goh′.

DEPARTING

Which is the way to the station?	Qual é o caminho para a estação?

kwal e oo kă-meen′-yoo pă-rah′ ish-tă-sow^{n}′.

Where is the train for ——?	Onde está o comboio para...?

o^{n}d ish-ta′ oo ko^{n}-boy′-yoo pă′-ră...

When does the train for —— leave?	Quando parte o comboio para...?

kwa^{n}′-doo part oo ko^{n}-boy′-yoo pă′-ră...

From which platform?	De que plataforma?

dĕ kĕ plă-tă-for′-mă.

Which is the way to platform number ——?	Por onde se vai à plataforma número...?

poor o^{n}d sĕ vȳ ah plă-tă-for′-mă noo′-mĕ-roo...

Where is the booking-office?	Onde é a bilheteira?

o^{n}d′-ee e ă beel-yĕ-tay′-ee-ră.

Is it an express?	É rápido?

e ra′-pee-doo.

Is there a supplementary charge?	Paga-se excesso?

pah′-găs eesh-se′-soo.

How much extra does one pay?	Quanto mais se paga?

kwa^{n}′-too mȳsh sĕ pah′-gă.

Is this ticket valid for an express?	Este bilhete é válido para um rápido?

aysht beel-yet′ e va′-lee-doo pă′-ră oo^{n} ra′-pee-doo.

Is there a first, second, third class?	Há primeira, segunda, terceira classe?

ah prĕ-may′-ee-ră, sĕ-goo^{n}′-dă, tĕr-say′-ee-ră klas.

Is there a sleeping-car?	Há carruagem-cama?

ah kă-roo-ah′-zhe^{n} kă′-mă,

Can I reserve a seat, a sleeper?	Posso reservar um lugar, uma cama?

po′-soo rĕ-zĕr-var′ oo^{n} loo-gar′, oo′-mă kă′-mă.

Smoking, non-smoking.	Fumadores, não-fumadores.

foo-mă-doh′-rĕsh, now^{n} foo-mă-doh′-rĕsh.

In the front, middle, rear of the train.	À frente, ao meio, na cauda do comboio.

ah fre^{n}t, ow may′-yoo, nă kow′-dă doo ko^{n}-boy′-yoo.

Facing the engine.	Voltado para a máquina.

vohl-tah′-doo pă-rah′ ma′-kee-nă.

Back to the engine.	De costas para a máquina.

de kosh′-tăsh pă-rah′ ma′-kee-nă.

A window-seat.	Um lugar junto à janela.

oo^{n} loo-gar′ zhoo^{n}-too ah zhă-ne′-lă.

Are there any seats left?	Há ainda lugares?

ah ă-ee^{n}′-dă loo-garsh′.

First, second, third class return.	Um bilhete de ida e volta de primeira, segunda, terceira classe.

oo^{n} beel-yet′ dee′-dă ee vol′-tă dĕ prĕ-may′-ee-ră, sĕ-goo^{n}′-dă, tĕr-say′-ee-ră klas.

Single to ——	Bilhete de ida para...

beel-yet′ dee′-dă pă′-ră...

Three returns to ——	Três idas e voltas para...

trayz ee′-dăz ee vol′-tăsh pă′-ră...

Two singles to ——	Dois bilhetes para...

doh′-eezh beel-yetsh′ pă′-ră...

Please write down the price.	Faz favor de marcar o preço.

fash fă-vohr′ dĕ măr-kar′ oo pray′-soo.

Where can I get a platform-ticket?	Onde posso comprar um bilhete-de-gare?

o^{n}d po′-soo ko^{n}-prar′ oo^{n} beel-yet′ dĕ gar.

Upper (lower) berth.	Cama de cima (de baixo).

kă′-mă dĕ see′-mă, dĕ bȳ′-shoo.

We want to be alone if possible.	Queremos estar sòzinhos se for possível.

kĕ-ray′-mooz ish-tar′ so-zeen′-yoosh sĕ fohr poo-see′-vĕl.

I should like a pillow, a rug.	Desejava uma almofada, uma manta.

dĕ-zĕ-zhah′-vă oom al-moo-fah′-dă, oo′-mă ma^{n}′-tă.

What time is breakfast, lunch, tea, dinner?	A que horas é o pequeno almoço, o almoço, o chá, o jantar?

ă kee o′-răz e oo pĕ-kay′-noo al-moh′-soo, oo al-moh′-soo, oo shah, oo zha^{n}-tar′.

When do we arrive?	Quando chegamos?

kwa^{n}′-doo shĕ-gă′-moosh.

Wake me at ——	Acorde-me às...

ă-kord′-ĕ mĕ ash...

I should like tea, coffee, in the morning.	Queria chá, café, de manhã.

kĕ-ree′-ă shah, kă-fe′, dĕ măn-ya^{n}′.

I should like some hot water.	Queria água quente.

kĕ-ree′-ă ag′-wă ke^{n}t.

I should like a glass, jug, of water.	Queria um copo, um jarro, de água.

kĕ-ree′-ă oo^{n} ko′-poo, oo^{n} zha′-roo, dag′-wă.

Drinking water.	Água filtrada.

ag′-wă feel-trah′-dă.

Luggage-van.	O furgão.

oo foor-gow^{n}′.

LUGGAGE

Porter. — Bagageiro.
bă-gă-zhay′-ee-roo.

Are you free? — Está livre?
ish-ta′ leevr.

Take my luggage. — Leve a minha bagagem.
lev ă meen′-yă bă-gah′-zhe^{n}.

Can you carry this case too? — Pode levar esta mala também?
pod lĕ-var′ esh′-tă ma′-lă tow^{n}-be^{n}′.

Be careful with this case. — Cuidado com esta mala.
kwee-dah′-doo ko^{n} esh′-tă ma′-lă.

I have some heavy luggage too. — Também tenho bagagem pesada.
tow^{n}-be^{n}′ ten′-yoo bă-gah′-zhe^{n} pĕ-zah′-dă.

Four pieces. — Quatro volumes.
kwat′-roo voo-loomsh′.

Left luggage office. — O depósito de volumes.
oo dĕ-po′-zee-too dĕ voo-loomsh′.

Where can I leave my luggage? — Onde posso guardar as malas?
o^{n}d po′-soo gwăr-dar′ ăzh ma′-lăsh.

Where can I register the luggage? — Onde posso despachar a bagagem?
o^{n}d po′-soo dish-pă-shar′ ă bă-gah′-zhe^{n}.

Can I take these things in the compartment with me? — Posso levar estas coisas no compartimento comigo?
po′-soo lĕ-var′ esh′-tăsh koh′-ee-zăzh noo ko^{n}-păr-tee-me^{n}′-too koo-mee′-goo.

Put them here. — Ponha-as aqui.
pohn′-yaz ă-kee′.

Trunk, case, brief-case, parcel, package, basket.	Mala grande, mala, pasta, pacote, embrulho, cesto.

ma′-lă gra^{n}d, ma′-lă, pash′-tă, pă-kot′, e^{n}-brool′-yoo, saysh′-too.

I want to send these cases in advance.	Quero mandar estas malas com antecedência.

kair′-oo ma^{n}-dar′ esh′-tăzh ma′-lăsh ko^{n} a^{n}-tĕ-sĕ-de^{n}′-see-ă.

I want to insure my luggage.	Quero segurar a minha bagagem.

kair′-oo sĕ-goo-rar′ ă meen′-yă bă-gah′-zhe^{n}.

What does it cost?	Quanto custa?

kwa^{n}′-too koosh′-tă.

It is not worth while.	Não vale a pena.

now^{n} val ă pay′-nă.

The receipt (for luggage).	A senha.

ă sen′-yă.

Where can I find you?	Onde o posso encontrar?

o^{n}d′-ee oo po′-soo e^{n}-ko^{n}-trar′.

Wait for me here.	Espere aqui por mim.

ish-pair′ ă-kee′ poor mee^{n}.

I am going to the refreshment-room.	Vou ao bufete.

voh ow boo-fet′.

I shall be back soon, in ten minutes.	Volto já, em dez minutos.

vol′-too zhah, e^{n} dezh mĕ-noo′-toosh.

I shall wait for you on the platform, at the entrance.	Espero-o na plataforma, à entrada.

ish-pair′-oo-oo nă plă-tă-for′-mă, ah e^{n}-trah′-dă.

AT THE LEFT-LUGGAGE

I wish to leave these things here.	Quero deixar estas coisas aqui.

kair′-oo day-ee-shar′ esh′-tăsh koh′-ee-zaz ă-kee′.

Until about four o'clock. | Até por volta das quatro.

ă-te' poor vol'-tă dăsh kwa'-troo.

Three cases, a raincoat, this parcel, these books. | Três malas, uma gabardina, este pacote, estes livros.

trayzh ma'-lăsh, oo'-mă gă-băr-dee'-nă, aysht pă-kot', ayshtzh leev'-roosh.

Those are my things over there. | As minhas coisas estão ali.

ăzh meen'-yăsh koh'-ee-zăz ish-tow^{n}' ă-lee'.

There is one case missing. | Falta uma mala.

fal'-tă oo'-mă ma'-lă.

Where is the parcel? | Onde está o pacote?

o^{n}d ish-ta' oo pă-kot'.

This is not mine. | Isto não é meu.

eesh'-too now^{n} e may'-oo.

I want to take out one suitcase. | Quero levar uma mala.

kair'-oo lĕ-var' oo'-mă ma'-lă.

The remainder can stay. | O resto pode ficar.

oo resh'-too pod fee-kar'.

How much is there to pay? | Quanto é?

kwa^{n}'-too e.

How much do you charge for each item? | Quanto custa cada objecto?

kwa^{n}'-too koosh'-tă kă'-dă ob-je'-too.

Do I pay now or when I collect the things? | Pago agora, ou quando levar as coisas?

pah'-goo ă-go'-ră, oh kwa^{n}'-doo lĕ-var' ăsh koh'-ee-zăsh.

This case is not locked. | Esta mala não está fechada à chave.

esh'-tă ma'-lă now^{n} ish-ta' fĕ-shah'-dă ah shahv.

The lock is broken. | A fechadura está quebrada.

ă fĕ-shă-doo'-ră ish-ta' kĕ-brah'-dă.

Something has fallen out. | Caiu qualquer coisa.

kă-yoo′ kwal′-kair koh′-ee-ză.

Please keep an eye on my things till I find a porter. | Faz favor de vigiar a minha bagagem enquanto procuro um bagageiro.

fash fă-vohr dĕ vee-zhee-ar′ ă meen′-yă bă-gah′-zhe^{n} e^{n}-kwa^{n}′-too proo-koo′-roo oo^{n} bă-gă-zhay′-ee-roo.

AT THE STATION, GENERAL

Booking-office. | A bilheteira.

ă beel-yĕ-tay′-ee-ră.

Enquiry-office. | Informações.

ee^{n}-foor-mă-soy^{n}sh′.

Left-luggage. | Depósito de volumes.

dĕ-po′-zee-too dĕ voo-loomsh′.

Waiting-room. | Sala de espera.

sa′-lă dish-pair′-ă.

Lost Property Office. | Depósito de objectos perdidos.

dĕ-po′-zee-too dob-zhe′-toosh pĕr-dee′-doosh.

Stationmaster. | Chefe de estação.

shef dish-tă-sow^{n}′.

Railway official, employee. | Empregado.

e^{n}-prĕ-gah′-doo.

Ladies, Gentlemen (W.C.). | Senhoras, Homens.

sĕn-yoh′-răsh, o′-me^{n}sh.

Bookstall. | Jornais, kiosque.

zhoor-nÿzh′, kee-oshk′.

Have you any English papers, books? | Tem jornais, livros, ingleses?

te^{n} zhoor-nÿsh′, leev′-roosh, ee^{n}-glay′-zĕsh.

These are old.	Estes são antigos.

aysh tsh sow^{n} a^{n}-tee′-goosh.

Can I post a letter here?	Posso deitar uma carta aqui?

po′-soo day-ee-tar′ oo′-mă kar′-tă ă-kee′.

Have you any post-cards?	Tem bilhetes postais?

te^{n} beel-yetsh′ poosh-tȳsh′.

Where can I get stamps?	Onde posso comprar selos?

o^{n}d po′-soo ko^{n}-prar′ say′-loosh.

Where can I send a telegram?	Onde posso mandar um telegrama.

o^{n}d po′-soo ma^{n}-dar′ oo^{n} tĕ-lĕ-gră′-mă.

Telephone-kiosk.	Cabine telefónica.

kă-been′ tĕ-lĕ-fo′-nee-kă.

TIME-TABLES

Where is the time-table?	Onde está o horário?

o^{n}d ish-ta′ oo oo-rah′-ree-oo.

Have you a time-table?	Tem um horário?

te^{n} oo^{n} oo-rah′-ree-oo.

Can you show me how to use this time-table?	Pode mostrar-me a maneira de consultar este horário?

pod moosh-trar′-mee ă mă-nay′-ee-ră dĕ ko^{n}-sool-tar′ aysht oo-rah′-ree-oo.

What does this sign mean?	Que quer dizer este sinal?

kĕ kair dee-zayr′ aysht see-nal′.

Week-days only.	Só nos dias úteis.

so noozh dee′-ăz oo′-tay-eesh.

Saturdays.	Sábados.

sa′-bă-doosh.

Sundays.	Domingos.

doo-mee^{n}′-goosh.

Holidays.	Feriados.

fĕ-ree-ah′-doosh.

ON THE TRAIN.

Is this seat free?	Este lugar está livre?

aysht loo-gar′ ish-ta′ leevr.

Is there room for two here?	Há aqui lugar para dois?

ah ă-kee′ loo-gar′ pă′-ră doh′-eesh.

That seat is taken.	Esse lugar está ocupado.

ays loo-gar′ ish-ta′ oo-koo-pah′-doo.

Put my luggage on the rack, under the seat.	Ponha a minha bagagem na rede, debaixo do banco.

poh′-nya meen′-yă bă-gah′-zhe^{n} nă rayd, dĕ-by′-shoo doo ba^{n}′-koo.

Excuse me (may I pass?)	Com licença.

ko^{n} lee-se^{n}′-să.

I am sorry to disturb you.	Desculpe incomodá-lo.

dish-koolp′ ee^{n}-koo-moo-da′-loo.

Are these things in your way?	Estas coisas incomodam?

esh′-tăsh koh′-ee-zăz ee^{n}-koo-mo′-dow^{n}.

No, it's quite all right.	Não, está bem.

now^{n}, ish-ta′ be^{n}.

Do you mind if I smoke?	Incomoda-o se fumar?

ee^{n}-koo-mo′-dă-oo se foo-mar′.

Can you give me a light, please?	Pode dar-me lume, se faz favor?

pod dar′-mĕ loom, sĕ fash fă-vohr′.

Would you like to look at the paper?	Quer ver o jornal?

kair vayr oo zhoor-nal′.

May I open the window? — Dá-me licença para abrir a janela?

da′-mĕ lee-se^{n}′-să pă′-ră ăb-reer′ ă zhă-ne′-lă.

Would you mind if I have the window closed? — Importa-se que feche a janela?

ee^{n}-por′-tăs kĕ fesh ă zhă-ne′-lă.

The window will not close, open. — A janela não fecha, abre.

ă zhă-ne′-lă now^{n} fay′-shă, ab′-rĕ.

The door is jammed. — É impossível abrir a porta.

e ee^{n}-poo-see′-vĕl ăb-reer′ ă por′-tă.

It is hot, cold. — Está quente, frio.

ish-ta′ ke^{n}t, free′-oo.

Do you feel a draught? — Sente uma corrente de ar?

se^{n}t oo′-mă koo-re^{n}t′ dar.

Is the sun troubling you? — O sol incomoda-o?

oo sol ee^{n}-koo-mo′-dă-oo.

We can draw the blind. — Podemos baixar as cortinas.

poo-day′-moozh bȳ-shar′ ăsh koor-tee′-năsh.

Is there a bell for the attendant? — Há uma campainha para chamar o empregado?

ah oo′-mă ka^{n}-pă-een′-yă pă′-ră shă-mar′ oo e^{n}-prĕ-gah′-doo.

I should like something to drink. — Desejava alguma coisa para beber.

dĕ-zĕ-zhah′-vă al-goo′-mă koh′-ee-ză pă′-ră bĕ-bayr′.

What are we stopping for? — Para quê paramos?

pă′-ră kay pă-ră′-moosh.

How much longer is it to ——? — Quanto demora até...?

kwa^{n}′-too dĕ-mo′-ra ă-te′...

Are we nearly at ——? — Estamos perto de...?

ish-tă′-moosh pair′-too dĕ...

Are we late? | Estamos atrasados?

ish-tă′-mooz ă-tră-zah′-doosh.

We are on time. | Vamos à tabela.

vă′-mooz ah tă-be′-lă.

Where are we now? | Onde estamos agora?

o^{n}d ish-tă′-mooz ă-go′-ră.

Do you know whether we pass through ——? | Sabe se passamos por...?

sab sĕ pă-să′-moosh poor...

Here is my ticket. | Aqui está o meu bilhete.

ă-kee′ ish-ta′ oo may′-oo beel-yet′.

To pull the communication cord. | Puxar o sinal de alarme.

poo-shar′ oo see-nal′ da-larm′.

TRAVELLING BY SEA

Shipping company. | Companhia de navegação.

ko^{n}-păn-yee′-ă dĕ nă-vĕ-gă-sow^{n}′.

Shipping agents. | Agência de navegação.

ă-zhe^{n}′-see-ă dĕ nă-vĕ-gă-sow^{n}′.

Can I book a passage to ——? | Posso reservar passagem para...?

po′-soo rĕ-zĕr-var′ pă-sah′-zhe^{n} pă′-ră...

First, second, class. | Primeira, segunda, classe.

prĕ-may′-ee-ră, sĕ-goo^{n}-dă, klas.

Tourist class. | Classe turística.

klas too-reesh′-tee-kă.

Third class. | Terceira classe.

tĕr-say′-ee-ră klas.

Sailing date. | Data da saída.

da′-tă dă să-ee′-dă.

Arrival date. | Data da chegada.

da′-tă dă shĕ-gah′-dă.

From which dock?	De que cais?
	dĕ kĕ kȳsh.
At what time do we embark?	A que horas embarcamos?
	ă kee o′-răz e^{n}-băr-kă′-moosh.
When do we sail?	Quando partimos?
	kwa^{n}′-doo păr-tee′-moosh.
Where do I get the tickets?	Onde compro os bilhetes?
	o^{n}d ko^{n}′-proo oozh beel-yetsh′.
Will you show me my cabin?	Pode indicar-me o meu camarote?
	pod ee^{n}-dee-kar′-mee oo may′-oo kă-mă-rot′.
Can I change my berth?	Posso mudar de beliche?
	po′-soo moo-dar′ dĕ bĕ-leesh′.
Which is the way on deck?	Por onde se vai à coberta?
	poor o^{n}d se vȳ ah koo-bair′-tă.
Which is the way below?	Por onde se vai lá para baixo?
	poor o^{n}d se vȳ lah pă′-ră by′-shoo.
Where is the dining-room?	Onde é a sala de jantar?
	o^{n}d′-ee e ă sa′-lă dĕ zha^{n}-tar′.
Where is the lounge, the bar?	Onde é o salão, o bar?
	o^{n}d′-ee e oo să-low^{n}′, oo bar.
Where is the purser's office?	Onde é o escritório?
	o^{n}d′-ee e oo ish-kree-to′-ree-oo.
When does it open?	Quando abre?
	kwa^{n}′-doo ab′-rĕ.
I want to change some money.	Quero cambiar dinheiro.
	kair′-oo ka^{n}-bee-ar′ deen-yay′-ee-roo.

I can't find my luggage. | Não encontro a minha bagagem.

now^{n} e^{n}-ko^{n}′-troo ă meen′-yă bă-gah′-zhe^{n}.

My luggage is not all here. | Não está aqui toda a minha bagagem.

now^{n} ish-ta′ ă-kee′ toh′-da meen′-yă bă-gah′-zhe^{n}.

A case, a package, is missing. | Falta uma mala, um pacote.

fal′-tă oo′-mă ma′-lă, oo^{n} pă-kot′.

Will you close the porthole? | Faz favor de fechar vigia.

fash fă-vohr′ dĕ fĕ-shar′ ă vĕ-zhee′-ă.

Is there a ventilator? | Há um ventilador?

ah oo^{n} ve^{n}-tee-lă-dohr′.

The fan does not work. | A ventoinha não funciona.

ă ve^{n}-too-een′-yă now^{n} foon-see-oh′-nă.

I need another pillow, blanket. | Preciso de outra almofada, outro cobertor.

prĕ-see′-zoo doh′-tră al-moo-fah′-dă, oh′-troo koo-bĕr-tohr′.

I need a towel, soap. | Preciso de uma toalha, de sabonete.

prĕ-see′-zoo doo′-mă too-al′-yă, dĕ să-boo-net′.

I need some drinking-water. | Preciso de água para beber.

prĕ-see′-zoo dag′-wă pă′-ră bĕ-bayr′.

I feel sick. | Sinto-me enjoado.

see^{n}′-too-mĕ e^{n}-zhoo-ah′-doo.

Bring a basin. | Traga uma bacia.

trah′-gă oo′-mă bă-see′-ă.

Bring me a brandy. | Traga um brandy.

trah′-gă oo^{n} bra^{n}′-dee.

Bring me something to drink. | Traga-me qualquer coisa para beber.

trah′-gă-mĕ kwal′-kair koh′-ee-ză pă′-ră bĕ-bayr′.

I feel better.	Sinto-me melhor.
see^n′-too-mĕ mĕl-yor′.	
I hope you will feel better.	Estimo as suas melhoras.
ish-tee′-moo ăsh soo′-ăzh mĕl-yor′-ăsh.	
I want a deck-chair.	Quero uma cadeira de lona.
kair′-oo oo′-mă kă-day′-ee-ră dĕ loh′-nă.	
What is the charge?	Quanto custa?
kwa^n′-too koosh′-tă.	
When does the ship reach ——?	Quando chega o barco a ...?
kwa^n′-doo shay′-gă oo bar′-koo ă...	
Can we go ashore in ——?	Podemos desembarcar em...?
poo-day′-moozh dĕ-ze^n-băr-kar′ e^n...	
Must I get a landing-ticket?	Preciso de um cartão de desembarque?
prĕ-see′-zoo doo^n kăr-tow^n′ dĕ dĕ-ze^n-bark′.	
Do we need to take our passports?	É preciso levar os passaportes?
e prĕ-see′-zoo lĕ-var′ oosh pa-să-portsh′.	
Are the passports examined on board?	Os passaportes são vistos a bordo?
oosh pa-să-portsh′ sow^n veesh′-tooz ă bor′-doo.	

TRAVELLING BY AIR

Where is the air travel agency?	Onde é a agência aérea?
o^{n}d′-ee e a-zhe^n′-see-ă ă-air′-ee-ă.	
Is there a plane from here to ——?	Há um avião de aqui para...?
ah oo^n ă-vee-ow^n′ dă-kee′ pă′-ră...	
When does the plane leave?	Quando parte o avião?
kwa^n′-doo part oo ă-vee-ow^n′.	

When do we reach ——? | Quando chegamos a...?
kwa^n′-doo shĕ-gă′-mooz ă...

Can I go direct? | Posso ir directamente?
po′-soo eer dee-re′-tă-me^{n}t.

Do we land anywhere before reaching ——? | Paramos em algum sítio antes de chegar a...?
pă-ră′-mooz e^n al-goo^n′ see′-tee-oo a^{n}tsh de shĕ-gar′ ă...

What is the fare, single, return? | Quanto é a passagem, ida, ida e volta?
kwa^n′-too e ă pă-sah′-zhe^n, ee′-dă, ee′-dă ee vol′-tă.

I want to reserve a seat in the plane for —— | Quero reservar um lugar no avião para...
kair′-oo rĕ-zĕr-var′ oo^n loo-gar′ noo ă-vee-ow^n′ pă′-ră...

How do I get to the airport? | Como se vai para o aeroporto?
koh′-moo sĕ vȳ pă′-ră oo air-oo-pohr′-too.

Is there transport? | Há transporte?
ah tra^{n}sh-port′.

I must cancel my reservation. | Tenho de cancelar a reserva de lugar.
ten′-yoo dĕ ka^n-sĕ-lar′ ă rĕ-zair′-vă dĕ loo-gar′.

How much luggage may I take? | Quanta bagagem posso levar?
kwa^n′-tă bă-gah′-zhe^n po′-soo lĕ-var′.

What is the charge? | Quanto custa?
kwa^n′-too koosh′-tă.

Can I change my seat? | Posso mudar de assento?
po′-soo moo-dar′ dă-se^n′-too.

I feel sick. | Sinto-me enjoado.
see^n′-too-mĕ e^n-zhoo-ah′-doo.

Bring me a paper-bag. | Dê-me um saco-de-papel.
day′-mee oo^n sa′-koo dĕ pă-pel′.

I suffer from air-sickness. | Enjôo no avião.
e^n-zhoh′-oo noo ă-vee-ow^n′.

It is the first time I have travelled by air. | É a primeira vez que viajo de avião.
e ă prĕ-may′-ee-ră vaysh kĕ vee-ah′-zhoo dă-vee-ow^{n}′.

No smoking. | Não fumar.
now^{n} foo-mar′.

Fasten safety-belts. | Apertar os cintos.
ă-pĕr-tar′ oosh see^{n}′-toosh.

Emergency exit. | Saída de emergência.
să-ee′-dă dee-mĕr-zhe^{n}′-see-ă.

CUSTOMS

Articles for personal use, a moderate amount of tobacco (500 *grams*), *a camera, bicycle, and cars and motor-cycles which have a "Carnet de Passages en Douane" are free from duty. The use of a cigarette-lighter requires a special licence obtainable for a small charge.*

Where is the customs? | Onde é a Alfândega?
o^{n}d′-ee e al-fa^{n}′-dĕ-gă.

Do we have to leave the train? | Temos de descer do comboio?
tay′-moozh dĕ dĕsh-sayr′ doo ko^{n}-boy′-yoo.

Where are the passports examined? | Onde são vistos os passaportes?
o^{n}d sow^{n} veesh′-tooz oosh pa-să-portsh′.

Here is my passport. | Aqui está o meu passaporte.
ă-kee′ ish-ta′ oo may′-oo pa-să-port′.

How much money have you? | Quanto dinheiro tem?
kwa^{n}′-too deen-yay′-ee-roo te^{n}.

I have —— pounds, escudos. | Tenho...libras, escudos.
ten′-yoo...lee′-brăsh, ish-koo′-doosh.

I have —— in travellers' cheques.	Tenho...em "travellers' cheques".
ten'-yoo...e^{n} "travellers' cheques".	
I am waiting for the customs-officer.	Estou à espera do funcionário.
ish-toh' ah ish-pair'-ă doo foo^{n}-see-oo-nah'-ree-oo.	
This is my luggage.	Esta é a minha bagagem.
esh'-tă e ă meen'-yă bă-gah'-zhe^{n}.	
These are all mine.	Tudo isto é meu.
too'-doo eesh'-too e may'-oo.	
Have you anything to declare?	Tem alguma coisa a declarar?
te^{n} al-goo'-mă koh'-ee-ză ă dĕ-klă-rar'.	
Please open your cases.	Faz favor de abrir as suas malas.
fash fă-vohr' dă-breer' ăsh soo'-ăzh ma'-lăsh.	
I can't open this case.	Não posso abrir esta mala.
now^{n} po'-soo ă-breer' esh'-tă ma'-lă.	
The lock is stuck.	A fechadura está estragada.
ă fĕ-shă-doo'-ră ish-ta' ish-tră-gah'-dă.	
For my personal use.	Para meu uso pessoal.
pă'-ră may'-oo oo'-zoo pĕ-soo-al'.	
I am a tourist.	Sou turista.
soh too-reesh'-tă	
I am here on holiday.	Estou aqui de férias.
ish-toh' ă-kee' dĕ fe'-ree-ăsh.	
It is a business visit.	É uma visita de negócios.
e oo'-mă vĕ-zee'-tă dĕ nĕ-go'-see-oosh.	
I am staying here for a fortnight.	Fico aqui quinze dias.
fee'-koo ă-kee' kee^{n}z dee'-ăsh.	
It has been used.	É já usado.
e zhah oo-zah'-doo.	

I have only bought a few things during my stay.	Comprei poucas coisas durante a minha visita.
kon-pray′-ee poh′-kăsh koh′-ee-zăzh doo-ra^{n}t′ ă meen′-yă vĕ-zee′-tă.	
Is this dutiable?	Isto paga direitos?
eesh′-too pah′-gă dee-ray′-ee-toosh.	
How much must I pay?	Quanto devo pagar?
kwa^{n}′-too day′-voo pă-gar′.	
Where do I pay?	Onde pago?
o^{n}d pah′-goo.	
Have you finished?	Já acabou?
zhah ă-kă-boh′.	
I cannot close the case now.	Já não posso fechar a mala.
zhah now^{n} po′-soo fĕ-shar′ ă ma′-lă.	
Have the cases been marked?	As malas já foram marcadas?
ăzh ma′-lăzh zhah foh′-row^{n} măr-kah′-dăsh.	
My luggage has been examined.	A minha bagagem já foi examinada.
ă meen′-yă bă-gah′-zhe^{n} zhah foh′-ee ee-ză-mee-nah′-dă.	
I am in a hurry.	Estou com muita pressa.
ish-toh′ ko^{n} mwee^{n}′-tă pre′-să.	

AT THE HOTEL or BOARDING-HOUSE

Particulars and prices of the rooms in hotels and boarding-houses are posted in the hall or entrance of each establishment as well as in the rooms. Prices in Portugal are very moderate by British standards. A small supplementary charge is made for meals served in rooms, except for breakfast. Accommodation is rarely hard to find. Lists of hotels and boarding-houses can be obtained from the "Casa de Portugal" in London or the S.N.I. in Lisbon.

Can you recommend a hotel, a boarding-house?	Pode recomendar um hotel, uma pensão?

pod rě-koo-me^{n}-dar′ oo^{n} oh-tel′, oo′-mă pe^{n}-sow^{n}′.

I want to be near the centre of the town.	Quero ficar perto do centro da cidade.

kair′-oo fee-kar′ pair′-too doo se^{n}′-troo dă see-dahd′.

I don't want to be in a noisy area.	Não quero ficar num sítio barulhento.

now^{n} kair′-oo fee-kar′ noo^{n} see′-tee-oo bă-rool-ye^{n}′-too.

Where is the reception-desk?	Onde é o escritório?

o^{n}d′-ee e oo ish-kree-to′-ree-oo.

Where is the manager?	Onde está o gerente?

o^{n}d ish-ta′ oo zhě-re^{n}t′.

Where is the porter?	Onde está o porteiro?

o^{n}d ish-ta′ oo poor-tay′-ee-roo.

Have you a room vacant?	Tem um quarto livre?

te^{n} oo^{n} kwar′-too leevr.

I should like a single room.	Desejava um quarto duma cama só.

dě-zě-zhah′-vă oo^{n} kwar′-too doo′-mă kă′-mă so.

A double room.	Um quarto de casal.
oo^{n} kwar′-too dĕ kă-zal′.	
A room for the children.	Um quarto para as crianças.
oo^{n} kwar′-too pă-rash′ kree-a^{n}′-săsh.	
A room with a bath.	Um quarto com banho
oo^{n} kwar′-too ko^{n} băn′-yoo.	
Full board.	Pensão completa.
pe^{n}-sow^{n}′ ko^{n}-ple′-tă.	
For one night only.	Só para uma noite.
so pă′-ră oo′-mă noh′-eet.	
For a week, perhaps longer.	Para uma semana, talvez mais.
pă′-ră oo′-mă sĕ-mă′-nă, tal-vayzh′ mȳsh.	
May I see the room?	Posso ver o quarto?
po′-soo vayr oo kwar′-too.	
What does it cost?	Quanto custa?
kwa^{n}′-too koosh′-tă.	
That is expensive.	É caro.
e kah′-roo.	
Have you anything cheaper?	Tem um quarto mais barato?
te^{n} oo^{n} kwar′-too mȳzh bă-rah′-too.	
This is too small.	É muito pequeno.
e mwee^{n}′-too pĕ-kay′-noo.	
I will take this room.	Fico com este quarto.
fee′-koo ko^{n} aysht kwar′-too.	
What is the number of the room?	Qual é o número do quarto?
kwal e oo noo′-mĕ-roo doo kwar′-too.	
Have you got my key?	Tem a minha chave?
te^{n} ă meen′-yă shahv.	
Is there a lift?	Tem elevador?
te^{n} ee-lĕ-vă-dohr′.	

Please send the luggage to our room.	Faz favor de mandar a bagagem ao nosso quarto.

fash fă-vohr′ dĕ ma^{n}-dar′ ă bă-gah′-zhe^{n} ow no′-soo kwar′-too.

The luggage is in the station, in the taxi.	A bagagem está na estação, no táxi.

ă bă-gah′-zhe^{n} ish-ta′ nă ish-tă-sow^{n}′, noo tak′-see.

Can I have a meal in my room?	Posso tomar uma refeição no quarto?

po′-soo too-mar′ oo′-mă rĕ-fay-sow^{n}′ noo kwar′-too.

Open the windows.	Abra as janelas.

abr azh zhă-ne′-lăsh.

How do I open this window?	Como se abre esta janela?

koh′-moo see abr esh′-tă zhă-ne′-lă.

How do I draw these curtains?	Como posso fechar estas cortinas?

koh′-moo po′-soo fĕ-shar′ esh′-tăsh koor-tee′-năsh.

Where have you put our things?	Onde meteu as nossas coisas?

o^{n}d mĕ-tay′-oo ăzh no′-săsh koh′-ee-zăsh.

Where is the bell?	Onde está a campainha?

o^{n}d ish-ta′ ă ka^{n}-pă-een′-yă.

Where is the bathroom, lavatory?	Onde é a casa de banho, a toilette?

o^{n}d′-ee e ă kah′-ză dĕ băn′-yoo, ă twa-let′.

Where is the lounge, dining-room, bar?	Onde é o salão, a sala de jantar, o bar?

o^{n}d′-ee e oo să-low^{n}′, ă sa′-lă dĕ zha^{n}-tar′, oo bar.

I am going out now.	Eu saio já.

ay′-oo sȳ′-yoo zhah.

I shall be back for lunch, for dinner.	Volto para o almoço, o jantar.

vol′-too pă′-ră oo al-moh′-soo, oo zha^{n}-tar′.

Do you serve tea? | Servem chá?
sair′-ve^{n} shah.

Please bring some soap, a towel, hot water. | Faz favor de trazer sabonete, uma toalha, água quente.
fash fă-vohr dĕ tră-zayr′ să-boo-net′, oo′-mă too-al′-yă, ag′-wă ke^{n}t.

Please get me a bath ready. | Faz favor de me preparar banho.
fash fă-vohr′ dĕ mĕ prĕ-pă-rar′ băn′-yoo.

Call me at —— | Chame-me às...
sham′-ĕ-mĕ ash...

Good night. | Boa noite.
boh′-ă noh′-eet.

Good morning. | Bom dia.
bo^{n} dee′-ă.

Who is there? | Quem está aí?
ke^{n} ish-tah′ ă-ee′.

Come in. | Entre.
e^{n}′-trĕ.

What time is it? | Que horas são?
kee o′-răsh sow^{n}.

Wait a minute. | Espere um momento.
ish-pair′ oo^{n} moo-me^{n}′-too.

Can I have my shoes cleaned? | Pode limpar os meus sapatos?
pod lee^{n}-par′ oozh may′-oosh să-pah′-toosh.

I should like my clothes brushed, pressed. | Queria que escovem, que passem a ferro, a minha roupa.
kĕ-ree′-ă kee ish-ko′-ve^{n}, kĕ pa′-se^{n} ă fe′-roo, ă meen′-yă roh′-pă.

I have some things to be washed. | Tenho algumas coisas para lavar.
ten′-yoo al-goo′-măsh koh′-ee-zăsh pă′-ră lă-var′.

Are there any letters for me?	Há correspondência para mim?
ah koo-rěsh-po^{n}-de^{n}′-see-ă pă′-ră mee^{n}.	
Has anyone asked for me?	Perguntou alguém por mim?
pěr-goo^{n}-toh′ al-ge^{n}′ poor mee^{n}.	
Did anyone telephone for me?	Telefonou-me alguém?
tě-lě-foo-noh′-mee al-ge^{n}′.	
I want to post a letter.	Quero mandar uma carta.
kair′-oo ma^{n}-dar′ oo′-mă kar′-tă.	
Have you any stamps?	Tem selos?
te^{n} say′-loosh.	
I want to go to ——	Quero ir a...
kair′-oo eer ă...	
How do I get there?	Como se vai lá?
koh′-moo sě vȳ lah.	
Can I get something to eat (drink) when I return?	Posso comer (beber) alguma coisa ao voltar?
po′-soo koo-mayr′ (bě-bayr′) al-goo′-mă koh′-ee-ză ow vohl-tar′.	
Is there a night-porter on duty?	Há porteiro de serviço de noite?
ah poor-tay′-ee-roo dě sěr-vee′-soo dě noh′-eet.	
Is —— still in his (her) room?	...está ainda no seu quarto?
...ish-tah′ ă-ee^{n}′-dă noo say′-oo kwar′-too.	
What is the number of the room?	Qual é o número do quarto?
kwal e oo noo′-mě-roo doo kwar′-too.	
Will you send a message to him (her)?	É capaz de lhe mandar um recado?
e kă-pazh′ dě lyě ma^{n}-dar′ oo^{n} rě-kah′-doo.	

I should like some tickets for the cinema, theatre.	Queria bilhetes para o cinema, o teatro.

kĕ-ree′-ă beel-yetsh′ pă′-ră oo see-naym′-ă, oo tee-ah′-troo.

What time does it begin?	A que horas começa?

ă kee o′-răsh koo-me′-să.

Push.	Empurrar.

e^{n}-poo-rar′.

Pull.	Puxar.

poo-shar′.

Press (bell), press (button).	Tocar, carregar.

too-kar′, kă-rĕ-gar′.

Maid	A criada

ă kree-ah′-dă

LEAVING THE HOTEL

I wish to pay my bill.	Queria pagar a minha conta.

kĕ-ree′-ă pă-gar′ ă meen′-yă ko^{n}′-tă.

How much is it?	Quanto é?

kwa^{n}′-too e.

What are these charges for?	Do que são estas verbas?

doo kĕ sow^{n} esh′-tăzh vair′-băsh.

I think there is a mistake here.	Creio que há um engano aqui.

kray′-yoo kee ah oo^{n} e^{n}-gă′-noo ă-kee′.

I did not have ——	Não tomei...

now^{n} too-may′-ee...

You said the rooms cost ——	Disse que os quartos custavam...

dees kee oosh kwar′-toosh koosh-tah′-vow^{n}...

May I have the receipt?	Pode dar-me o recibo?

pod dar′-mee oo rĕ-see′-boo.

Do I tip, or is there a charge for service in the bill? | Devo dar uma gorjeta, ou está incluido o serviço na conta?

day′-voo dar oo′-mă goor-zhay′-tă, oh ish-ta′ ee^{n}-kloo-ee′-doo oo sĕr-vee′-soo nă ko^{n}′-tă.

I am leaving tomorrow, to-night, this afternoon. | Parto amanhã, esta noite, esta tarde.

par′-too a-măn-ya^{n}′, esh′-tă noh′-eet, esh′-tă tard.

Have my luggage brought down. | Mande buscar a minha bagagem.

ma^{n}d boosh-kar′ ă meen′-yă bă-gah′-zhe^{n}.

Send the luggage to the station. | Mande a bagagem à estação.

ma^{n}d ă bă-gah′-zhe^{n} ah ish-tă-sow^{n}′.

How soon should I leave? | Quando devo partir?

kwa^{n}′-doo day′-voo păr-teer′.

How long does it take to the station, the dock, the airport? | Quanto tempo leva para ir à estação, ao cais, ao aeroporto?

kwa^{n}′-too te^{n}′-poo le′-vă pă′-ră eer ah ish-tă-sow^{n}′, ow kȳsh, ow air-oo-pohr′-too.

Can I walk? | Posso ir a pé?

po′-soo eer ă pe.

Please get a taxi. | Faz favor de chamar um táxi.

fash fă-vohr dĕ shă-mar′ oo^{n} tak′-see.

Have you any labels? | Tem etiquetas?

te^{n} e-tee-kay′-tăsh.

I should like some food for the journey. | Desejava qualquer coisa de comer para a viagem.

dĕ-zĕ-zhah′-vă kwal′-kair koh′-ee-ză dĕ koo-mayr′ pă-rah′ vee-ah′-zhe^{n}.

When must I leave my room? | Quando devo desocupar o meu quarto?

kwa^{n}′-doo day′-voo dĕ-zoo-koo-par′ oo may′-oo kwar′-too.

Can I leave my luggage here?	Posso deixar a minha bagagem aqui?

po′-soo day-ee-shar′ ă meen′-yă bă-gah′-zhe^n ă-kee′.

I have been very comfortable.	Estive bem instalado.

ish-teev′ be^n ee^{n}sh-tă-lah′-doo.

If any letters come for me, please send them to this address:—	Se vier correspondência para mim, faz favor de mandá-la para esta direcção....

sĕ vee-air′ koo-rĕsh-po^n-de^n′-see-ă pă′-ră mee^n, fash fă-vohr dĕ ma^n-da′-lă pă′-ră esh′-tă dee-re-sow^n′...

LAUNDRY

For washing list see vocabulary under "SHOPPING", page 82. Washing is often done on the premises, effectively and expeditiously. Charges are not high.

I have some things to be washed.	Tenho algumas coisas para lavar.

ten′-yoo al-goo′-măsh koh′-ee-zăsh pă′-ră lă-var′.

When will they be ready?	Quando estarão prontas?

kwa^n′-doo ish-tă-row^n′ pro^n′-tăsh.

Can they be ready tomorrow, in two days?	Podem estar prontas amanhã, depois de amanhã?

po′-de^n ish-tar′ pro^n′-taz a-măn-ya^n′, dĕ-poh′-eezh da-măn-ya^n′.

I leave on ——	Parto...

par′-too...

I should like these things back soon.	Queria ter estas coisas cedo.

kĕ-ree′-ă tayr esh′-tăsh koh′-ee-zăsh say′-doo.

Be very careful with these things. | Tenha muito cuidado com estas coisas.

ten′-yă mwee^{n}′-too kwee-dah′-doo ko^{n} esh′-tăsh koh′-ee-zăsh.

Don't starch the collars. | Não engome os colarinhos.

now^{n} e^{n}-gom′ oosh koo-lă-reen′-yoosh.

Some of the things need mending. | Algumas coisas precisam de ser consertadas.

al-goo′-măsh koh′-ee-zăsh prĕ-see′-zow^{n} dĕ sayr ko^{n}-sĕr-tah′-dăsh.

Can you arrange to have them mended for me? | Pode mandá-las consertar?

pod ma^{n}-da′-lăsh ko^{n}-sĕr-tar′.

There are —— missing. | Faltam...

fal′-tow^{n}...

Can you send my laundry to this address if it isn't ready in time? | Pode mandar a minha roupa para esta direcção se não estiver pronta a tempo?

pod ma^{n}-dar′ ă meen′-yă roh′-pă pă′-ră esh′-tă dee-re-sow^{n}′ sĕ now^{n} ish-tee-vair′ pro^{n}′-tă ă te^{n}′-poo.

LOCAL TOURS, EXCURSIONS

FINDING THE WAY

I want a guide book, a map, of the city. | Quero um roteiro, um mapa, da cidade.
kair′-oo oo^{n} roh-tay′-ee-roo, oo^{n} ma′-pă, dă see-dahd′.

Have you one in English? | Tem uma edição em inglês?
te^{n} oo′-mă ee-dee-sow^{n}′ e^{n} ee^{n}-glaysh′.

Could you tell me the way to ——? | Podia indicar-me o caminho para...?
poo-dee′-ă ee^{n}-dee-kar′-mee oo kă-meen′-yoo pă′-ră...

Is this the right way to ——? | Vou bem para...?
voh be^{n} pă′-ră...

How do I get from here to ——? | Como se vai daqui a...?
koh′-moo sĕ vȳ dă-kee′ ă...

I want to go to —— | Quero ir a...
kair′-oo eer ă...

I am looking for —— | Procuro...
proo-koo′-roo...

Is it far? | É longe?
e lo^{n}zh.

What distance is it? | Qual é a distância?
kwal e ă deesh-ta^{n}′-see-ă.

How long does it take? | Quanto tempo leva?
kwa^{n}′-too te^{n}′-poo le′-vă.

Is it better to go by taxi, tram, bus? | É preferível ir de táxi, de eléctrico, de autocarro?
e prĕ-fĕ-ree′-vĕl eer dĕ tak′-see, dee-le′-tree-koo, dow-too-ka′-roo.

Where is the tram stop, bus stop? | Onde é a paragem do eléctrico, do autocarro?

o^{n}d'-ee e ă pă-rah'-zhe^{n} doo ee-le'-tree-koo, doo ow-too-ka'-roo.

Does this bus, train, go to ——? | Este autocarro, eléctrico, vai para...?

aysht ow-too-ka'-roo, ee-le'-tree-koo, vȳ pă'-ră...

Is this the terminus? | É a última paragem?

e ă ool'-tee-mă pă-rah'-zhe^{n}.

Do I have to change? | Devo mudar?

day'-voo moo-dar'.

Straight ahead. | Sempre em frente.

se^{n}pr e^{n} fre^{n}t.

To the right, left. | À direita, à esquerda.

ah dee-ray'-ee-tă, ah ish-kayr'-dă.

First turning on the right. | A primeira travessa à direita.

ă prĕ-may'-ee-ră tră-ve'-să ah dee-ray'-ee-tă.

Second turning on the left. | A segunda travessa à esquerda.

ă sĕ-goo^{n}'-dă tră-ve'-să ah ish-kayr'-dă.

GOING BY CAR

I want to hire a car. | Quero alugar um automóvel.

kair'-oo ă-loo-gar' oo^{n} ow-too-mo'-vĕl.

I want to go by car. | Quero ir de automóvel.

kair'-oo eer dow-too-mo'-vĕl.

Is there a driver who speaks English? | Há um motorista que fale inglês?

ah oo^{n} moo-too-reesh'-tă kĕ fal ee^{n}-glaysh'.

What does it cost? | Quanto custa?

kwa^{n}'-too koosh'-tă.

How many kilometres is it? | Quantos quilómetros são?

kwa^{n}'-toosh kee-lo'-mĕ-troosh sow^{n}.

How long does it take?	Quanto tempo leva?

kwa^{n}′-too te^{n}-poo le′-vă.

I must be back by ——	É preciso estar de volta às...

e prĕ-see′-zoo ish-tar dĕ vol′-tă ash...

SIGHT-SEEING

Is there an English-speaking guide?	Há um guia que fale inglês?

ah oo^{n} gee′-ă kĕ fal ee^{n}-glaysh′.

I want to see all that is worth seeing.	Quero ver tudo quanto valha a pena ver.

kair′-oo vayr too′-doo kwa^{n}′-too val′-ya pay′-nă vayr.

At what time does the excursion start (end)	A que horas começa (termina) a excursão?

ă kee o′-răsh koo-may′-să (tĕr-mee′-nă) ă ish-koor-sow^{n}′

I have only two hours to spare.	Só tenho duas horas disponíveis.

so ten′-yoo doo′-ăz o′-răzh dish-poo-nee′-vay-eesh.

Have we time to see ——?	Temos tempo para ver ...?

tay′-moosh te^{n}′-poo pă′-ră vayr...

What street, church, is this?	Que rua, igreja, é esta?

kĕ roo′-ă, ee-gray′-zhă, e esh′-tă.

What building is that?	Que edifício é esse?

kee ĕ-dee-fee′-see-oo e ays.

What is that?	Que é isso?

kee e ee′-soo.

I am interested in art-galleries, museums.	Tenho interesse nos museus de arte, museus históricos.

ten′-yoo ee^{n}-tĕ-rays′ noozh moo-zay′-oozh dart, moo-zay′-ooz eesh-to′-ree-koosh.

I want to see the cathedral, the town hall, the university, the Roman remains, the tiled walls.	Quero ver a catedral, o município, a universidade, as ruinas romanas, os azulejos.

kair′-oo vayr ă kă-tĕ-dral′, oo moo-nee-see′-pee-oo, a oo-nee-vĕr-see-dahd′, ăzh roo-ee′-năzh roo-mă′-năsh, ooz ă-zoo-lay′-zhoosh.

I should like to visit the botanical gardens, the zoo.	Queria visitar o jardim botânico, o jardim zoológico.

kĕ-ree′-ă vĕ-zee-tar′ oo zhăr-dee^{n}′ boo-tă′-nee-koo, oo zhăr-dee^{n}′ zoo-oo-lo′-zhee-koo.

Is it worth getting out?	Vale a pena sair?

val ă pay′-nă să-eer′.

Wait here.	Espere aqui.

ish-pair′ ă-kee′.

Is it open?	Está aberto.

ish-ta′ ă-bair′-too.

When does it open, close?	Quando abre, fecha?

kwa^{n}′-doo ab′-rĕ, fay′-shă.

Can one see over the church, the castle?	Pode-se visitar a igreja, o castelo?

pod′-sĕ vĕ-zee-tar′ ă ee-gray′-zhă, oo kăsh-te′-loo.

To whom does one apply for permission to enter?	A quem se pede licença para entrar?

ă ke^{n} sĕ ped lee-se^{n}′-să pă′-ră e^{n}-trar′.

Can we go round alone?	Podemos ir sòzinhos?

poo-day′-mooz eer so-zeen′-yoosh.

Do we need a guide?	Precisamos dum guia?

prĕ-see-ză′-moozh doo^{n} gee′-ă.

When does the next tour start?	Quando começa a próxima visita?

kwa^{n}′-doo koo-me′-să ă pro′-see-mă vĕ-zee′-tă.

How long does it take?	Quanto tempo leva?

kwa^{n}′-too te^{n}′-poo le′-vă.

How long must we wait?	Quanto tempo temos de esperar?

kwa^{n}′-too te^{n}′-poo tay′-moozh dish-pě-rar′.

I am not interested in that.	Isso não me interessa.

ee′-soo now^{n} mě ee^{n}-tě-re′-să.

How much farther have we to go?	Até onde devemos ir?

ă-te′ o^{n}d dě-vay′-mooz eer.

How many rooms, steps, are there?	Quantas salas, quantos degraus, há?

kwa^{n}′-tăsh sa′-lăsh, kwa^{n}′-toozh dě-growsh′, ah.

Is there a good view?	Há uma boa vista?

ah oo′-mă boh′-ă veesh′-tă.

May I take a photograph here?	Posso tirar uma fotografia aqui?

po′-soo tee-rar′ oo′-mă foh-too-gră-fee′-ă ă-kee′.

Please stop a moment.	Faz favor de parar um momento.

fash fă-vohr′ dě pă-rar′ oo^{n} moo-me^{n}′-too.

Is this the —— memorial?	Este é o monumento de ...?

aysh′-tee e oo moh-noo-me^{n}′-too dě...

Where is —— buried?	Onde está enterrado...?

o^{n}d ish-ta′ e^{n}-tě-rah′-doo...

Where did —— live?	Onde morava...?

o^{n}d moo-rah′-vă...

What is the name of that?	Como se chama isso?

koh′-moo sě shă′-mă ee′-soo.

How much is the catalogue?	Quanto custa o catálogo?

kwa^{n}′-too koosh′-tă oo kă-ta′-loo-goo.

Can I buy any picture-postcards?	Posso comprar postais ilustrados?

po′-soo ko^{n}-prar′ poosh-tȳz′ ee-loosh-trah′-doosh

Have you a book about ——? | Tem um livro sobre...?

te^{n} oo^{n} leev′-roo soh′-brĕ...

Does one have to walk? | É preciso ir a pé?

e prĕ-see′-zoo eer ă pe.

Is it close by? | É perto?

e pair′-too.

Let us go. | Vamos.

vă′-moosh.

I am tired. | Estou cansado.

ish-toh′ ka^{n}-sah′-doo.

Let us rest a bit. | Vamos descansar um pouco.

vă′-moozh dĕsh-ka^{n}-sar′ oo^{n} poh′-koo.

It is too hot. | Faz muito calor.

fazh mwee^{n}′-too kă-lohr′.

I have seen enough for to-day. | Já vi bastante por hoje.

zhah vee băsh-ta^{n}t′ poor ohzh.

Where can I get some refreshments? | Onde posso tomar uns refrescos?

o^{n}d po′-soo too-mar′ oo^{n}zh rĕ-fraysh′-koosh.

It is going to rain. | Vai chover.

vȳ shoo-vayr′.

Where can we shelter? | Onde podemos encontrar abrigo?

o^{n}d poo-day′-mooz e^{n}-ko^{n}-trar′ ă-bree′-goo.

Can we get a taxi? | Podemos tomar um táxi?

poo-day′-moosh too-mar′ oo^{n} tak′-see.

Which is the best way back? | Qual é o melhor caminho de regresso?

kwal e oo mĕl-yor′ kă-meen′-yoo dĕ rĕ-gre′-soo.

Drive through —— | Vá por...

va poor...

Drive back as quickly as possible.	Volte o mais depressa possível.

volt oo mȳzh dĕ-pre′-să poo-see′-vĕl.

How much ought I to give the guide?	Quanto devo dar ao guia?

kwa^{n}′-too day′-voo dar ow gee′-ă.

Thank you very much.	Muito obrigado.

mwee^{n}t oh-bree-gah′-doo.

Are you free tomorrow?	Está livre amanhã?

ish-ta′ leevr a-măn-ya^{n}′.

Can you come at ten?	Pode vir às dez?

pod veer azh desh.

VISITING FRIENDS

I am looking for number —— | Procuro o número...

proo-koo′-roo oo noo′-mĕ-roo...

Does Mr. Costa live here? | O senhor Costa mora aqui?

oo sĕn-yohr′ kosh′-tă mo′-ră ă-kee′.

Is he at home? | Está em casa?

ish-ta′ e^n kah′-ză.

I am —— | Eu sou...

ay′-oo soh...

Tell him it is —— | Diga-lhe que é...

dee′-gă-lyĕ kee e...

Here is my card. | Aqui está o meu cartão.

a-kee′ ish-ta′ oo may′-oo kăr-tow^n′.

Please come in. | Faz favor de entrar.

fash fă-vohr′ de^n-trar′.

He will be in at —— | Volta às...

vol′-tă ash...

He won't be long. | Não deve tardar muito.

now^n dev tăr-dar′ mwee^n′-too.

Could you come back at —— | Podia voltar às...?

poo-dee′-ă vohl-tar′ ash...

Would you please wait a moment. | Tenha a bondade de esperar um momento.

ten′-ya bo^n-dahd′ dish-pĕ-rar′ oo^n moo-me^n′-too.

Please tell him I called. | Faz favor de dizer-lhe que eu estive aqui.

fash fă-vohr dĕ dee-zayr′-lyĕ kee ay′-oo ish-teev′ ă-kee′.

Mr. —— asked me to call on you.	O senhor...pediu-me para visitar V. Exª.

oo sĕn-yohr'...pĕ-dee'-oo-mĕ pă'-ră vĕ-zee-tar' vos-esh-sĕ-le^n'-see-ă.

How do you do?	Muito prazer (em conhecê-lo).

mwee^n'-too pră-zayr' (e^n koon-yĕ-say'-loo).

I speak very little Portuguese.	Falo pouco português.

fa'-loo poh'-koo poor-too-gaysh'.

Do you speak English, French, Spanish?	V. Exª. fala inglês, francês, espanhol?

vos-esh-sĕ-le^n'-see-ă fa'-lă ee^n-glaysh', fra^n-saysh', ish-păn-yol'.

I believe —— has mentioned my name to you.	Creio que...já lhe mencionou o meu nome.

kray'-yoo kĕ...zha lyĕ me^n-see-oo-noh' oo may'-oo nohm.

I have a letter of introduction.	Tenho uma carta de apresentação.

ten'-yoo oo'-mă kar'-tă dă-prĕ-ze^n-tă-sow^n'.

He is a great friend of mine.	É muito meu amigo.

e mwee^n'-too may'-oo ă-mee'-goo.

I have known him for a long time.	Conheço-o desde há muito tempo.

koon-yay'-soo-oo dezh'-dee ah mwee^n'-too te^n'-poo.

I knew him in ——	Conheci-o em...

koon-yĕ-see'-oo e^n...

He sends you his greetings.	Manda-lhe cumprimentos.

ma^n'-dă-lyĕ koo^n-pree-me^n'-toosh.

May I introduce ——?	Dá-me licença para apresentar...?

da'-mĕ lee-se^n'-să pă'-ră ă-prĕ-ze^n-tar'...

My wife, my husband, my son, my daughter, my friend. | Minha mulher, meu marido, meu filho, minha filha, meu amigo.
meen′-yă mool-yair′, may′-oo mă-ree′-doo, may′-oo feel′-yoo, meen′-yă feel′-yă, may′-oo ă-mee′-goo.

My uncle, aunt. | Meu tio, minha tia.
may′-oo tee′-oo, meen′-yă tee′-ă.

My nephew, niece. | Meu sobrinho, minha sobrinha.
may′-oo soo-breen′-yoo, meen′-yă soo-breen′-yă

My cousin (male, female). | Meu primo, minha prima.
may′-oo pree′-moo, meen′-yă pree′-mă

My brother-in-law, sister-in-law. | Meu cunhado, minha cunhada.
may′-oo koon-yah′-doo, meen′-yă koon-yah′-dă.

Could you come at ——? | Podia vir às...?
poo-dee′-ă veer ash...

I should like to very much. | Teria muito prazer.
tĕ-ree′-ă mwee^{n}′-too pră-zayr′.

I shall come to the hotel, boarding-house. | Eu irei ao hotel, à pensão.
ay′-oo ee-ray′-ee ow oh-tel′, ah pe^{n}-sow^{n}′.

Please do not go to any trouble. | Não se incomode.
now^{n} see ee^{n}-koo-mod′.

I hope it is not inconvenient. | Espero que não seja inoportuno.
ish-pair′-oo kĕ now^{n} say′-zhă ee-noo-poor-too′-noo.

Here is the address. | Aqui está a direcção.
ă-kee′ ish-ta′ ă dee-re-sow^{n}′.

I shall be glad to help you, accompany you, invite you. | Terei muito prazer em ajudá-lo ,acompanhá-lo, convidá-lo.
tĕ-ray′-ee mwee^{n}′-too pră-zayr′ e^{n} ă-zhoo-da′-loo, ă-ko^{n}-păn-ya′-loo, ko^{n}-vee-da′-loo.

Good-bye.	Adeus.
ă-day′-oosh.	
Until later.	Até logo.
ă-te′ lo′-goo.	
Until we meet again.	Até à vista.
ă-te′ ah veesh′-tă.	
Until tomorrow.	Até amanhã.
ă-te′ a-măn-ya^{n}′.	

SHOPPING

Shops are generally open from 9 a.m. to 1 p.m. and from 3 p.m. to 7 p.m. every day except Sunday. Newsagents and tobacconists close later. Sizes and weights are different from those used in Britain since Portugal uses the metric system. 1 inch is rather less than $2\frac{1}{2}$ centimetres; 1 metre is just under 40 inches; a kilogram is about 2 lb. 3 oz. (Some equivalent figures in the metric system are given on page 137). In shoes, a size 39 is a British size 6, 37 is a British size 5.

Very useful shopping information can be found regularly in the Anglo-Portuguese News, *which is published fortnightly in Lisbon.*

TOBACCONIST

British and American brands are plentiful and cheaper than in Britain. Portuguese cigarettes are cheaper still.

I want some cigarettes. | Quero cigarros.
kair′-oo see-ga′-roosh.

A packet of cigarettes. | Um maço de cigarros.
oo^{n} ma′-soo dĕ see-ga′-roosh.

Cigars, pipe tobacco. | Charutos, tabaco.
shă-roo′-toosh, tă-ba′-koo.

Have you British, American cigarettes? | Tem cigarros ingleses, americanos?
te^{n} see-ga′-rooz ee^{n}-glay′-zĕsh, ă-mĕ-ree-kă′-noosh.

How much are they? | Quanto custam?
kwa^{n}′-too koosh′-tow^{n}.

Have you a cheaper brand? | Tem outra marca mais barata?
te^{n} oh′-tră mar′-kă mӯzh bă-rah′-tă.

I shall take these. | Levo estes.
le′-voo ayshtsh.

Have you any matches? | Tem fósforos?
te^{n} fosh′-foo-roosh.

Cigarette-case. | Cigarreira.
see-gă-ray′-ee-ră.

Cigarette-holder. | Boquilha.
boo-keel′-yă.

Lighter, fuel. | Isqueiro, gasolina.
ish-kay′-ee-roo, gă-zoo-lee′-nă.

Flint, wick. | A pedra, a mecha.
ă ped′-ră, ă me′-shă.

Pipe, pipe-cleaner. | O cachimbo, o limpa-cachimbo.
oo kă-shee^{n}′-boo, oo lee^{n}′-pă kă-shee^{n}′-boo.

THE POST-OFFICE

Where is the main post-office? | Onde é o correio geral?
o^{n}d′-ee e oo koo-ray′-yoo zhĕ-ral′.

I want to send this letter by air-mail. | Quero mandar esta carta por avião.
kair′-oo ma^{n}-dar′ esh′-tă kar′-ta poor ă-vee-ow^{n}′.

What stamp is needed for this letter, this post-card? | Qual é a franquia para esta carta, este bilhete postal?
kwal e ă fra^{n}-kee′-ă pă′-ră esh′-tă kar′-tă, aysht beel-yet′ poosh-tal′.

By ordinary mail. | Por via normal.
poor vee′-ă nohr-mal′.

I want to send this parcel. | Quero mandar esta encomenda.
kair′-oo ma^{n}-dar′ esh′-tă e^{n}-koo-me^{n}′-dă.

This parcel is fragile. | Esta encomenda é frágil.
esh′-tă e^{n}-koo-me^{n}′-dă e fra′-zheel.

Which section do I go to? | A que guichet devo ir?
ă kĕ gee-shay′ day′-voo eer.

I want to register this letter, parcel.	Quero registar esta carta, encomenda.

kair′-oo rĕ-zheesh-tar′ esh′-tă kar′-tă, e^{n}-koo-me^{n}′-dă.

There is nothing dutiable in the package.	A encomenda não contém nada sujeito a direitos.

ă e^{n}-koo-me^{n}′-dă now^{n} ko^{n}-te^{n}′ nah′-dă soo-zhay′-ee-too ă dee-ray′-ee-toosh.

Letter-box, post-box.	A caixa do correio.

ă kȳ′-shă doo koo-ray′-yoo.

Inland mail; foreign mail; Portuguese overseas territories; Azores and Madeira.	Continente; Estrangeiro; Ultramar; Ilhas.

ko^{n}-tee-ne^{n}t′; ish-tra^{n}-zhay′-ee-roo; ool-tră-mar′; eel′-yăsh.

Air-mail.	Via aérea.

vee′-a air′-ee-ă.

I want to send a telegram.	Quero mandar um telegrama.

kair′-oo ma^{n}-dar′ oo^{n} tĕ-lĕ-gră′-mă.

Where are the telegram forms?	Onde estão os impressos para telegramas?

o^{n}d ish-tow^{n}′ ooz ee^{n}-pre′-soosh pă′-ră tĕ-lĕ-gră′-măsh.

Where is the Poste Restante?	Onde é a Posta-Restante?

o^{n}d′-ee e ă posh′-tă rĕsh-ta^{n}t′.

Have you any letters for me?	Tem cartas para mim?

te^{n} kar′-tăsh pă′-ră mee^{n}.

My name is ——	O meu nome é...

oo may′-oo nohm e...

My name is spelt like this ——	O meu nome escreve-se assim...

oo may′-oo nohm ish-krevs′ ă-see^{n}.

I am expecting a letter, parcel, from ——	Estou à espera duma carta, duma encomenda, de...

ish-toh′ ah ish-pair′-ă doo′-mă kar′-tă, doo′-mă e^{n}-koo-me^{n}′-dă, dĕ...

When does the last post go?	A que horas é a última tiragem do correio?

ă kee o′-răz e ă ool′-tee-mă tee-rah′-zhe^{n} doo koo-ray′-yoo.

Can you please post this letter for me?	Pode deitar-me esta carta?

pod day-ee-tar′-mee esh′-tă kar′-tă.

How much did it cost?	Quanto custou?

kwa^{n}′-too koosh-toh′.

THE CHEMIST

Is there a chemist near here?	Há uma farmácia perto de aqui?

ah oo′-mă făr-mah′-see-ă pair′-too dă-kee′.

Can you make up this prescription for me?	Pode aviar-me esta receita?

pod ă-vee-ar′-mee esh′-tă rĕ-say′-ee-tă.

I got this prescription in England.	Fizeram-me esta receita em Inglaterra.

fee-zair′-ow^{n}-mee esh′-tă rĕ-say′-ee-tă e^{n} ee^{n}-glă-te′-ră.

When will it be ready?	Quando estará pronta?

kwa^{n}′-doo ish-tă-ra′ pro^{n}′-tă.

Can you send it to ——?	Pode mandá-la a...?

pod ma^{n}-da′-lă ă...

Can you give me something for ——?	Pode dar-me alguma coisa para...?

pod dar′-mee al-goo′-mă koh′-ee-ză pă′-ră...

A chill, cold, sun-burn, headache.	Um resfriamento, uma constipação, queimadura do sol, dor de cabeça.

oo^{n} rĕsh-free-ă-me^{n}′-too, oo′-mă ko^{n}sh-tee-pă-sow^{n}′, kay-ee-mă-doo′-ră doo sol, dohr dĕ kă-bay′-să.

Constipation, diarrhoea, insect bites, indigestion.	Prisão de ventre, diarreia, picadas de insectos, indigestão.

pree-zow^{n}′ de ve^{n}tr, dee-ă-ray′-ya, pee-kah′-dăzh dee^{n}-se′-toosh, ee^{n}-dee-zhĕsh-tow^{n}′.

I want some antiseptic, aspirin.	Quero um antiséptico, aspirina.

kair′-oo oo^{n} a^{n}-tee-sep′-tee-koo, ăsh-pĕ-ree′-nă.

Cotton-wool, adhesive tape, lint, bandages.	Algodão em rama, adesivo, pensos, ligaduras.

al-goo-dow^{n}′ e^{n} ră′-mă, ă-dĕ-zee′-voo, pe^{n}′-soosh, lee-gă-doo′-răsh.

I have something in my eye.	Tenho qualquer coisa na vista.

ten′-yoo kwal′-kair koh′-ee-ză nă veesh′-tă.

I want some eye-lotion.	Quero uma loção para os olhos.

kair′-oo oo′-mă loh-sow^{n}′ pă′-ră ooz ol′-yoosh.

I feel sick, feverish.	Sinto-me doente, febril.

see^{n}′-too-mĕ doo-e^{n}t′, fĕ-breel′.

I feel faint, giddy.	Sinto-me a desmaiar, com vertigens.

see^{n}′-too-mee ă dĕzh-my-yar′, ko^{n} vĕr-tee′-zhe^{n}sh.

I don't feel well.	Não me sinto bem.

now^{n} mĕ see^{n}′-too be^{n}.

Can I speak to you privately?	Posso falar consigo em particular?

po′-soo fă-lar′ ko^{n}-see′-goo e^{n} păr-tee-koo-lar′.

May I speak to a male, female, assistant? | Posso falar com um empregado, uma empregada?

po′-soo fă-lar′ ko^{n} oo^{n} e^{n}-prĕ-gah′-doo, oo′-mă e^{n}-prĕ-gah′-dă.

I am being served. | Estão a servir-me.

ish-tow^{n}′ ă sĕr-veer′-mĕ.

I am waiting to speak to that lady, that gentleman. | Quero falar com essa senhora, esse senhor.

kair′-oo fă-lar′ ko^{n} e′-să sĕn-yohr′-ă, ay′-sĕ sĕn-yohr′.

Can you recommend a doctor? | Pode recomendar-me um médico?

pod rĕ-koo-me^{n}-dar′-mee oo^{n} me′-dee-koo.

Can you call a taxi? | Pode chamar um táxi?

pod shă-mar′ oo^{n} tak′-see.

I want something for my feet. | Quero uma coisa para os pés.

kair′-oo oo′-mă koh′-ee-ză pă′-ră oosh pesh.

Blisters, corns. | Borbulhas, calos.

boor-bool′-yăsh, ka′-loosh.

Bath salts. | Sais de banho.

sȳzh dĕ băn′-yoo.

Comb. | Um pente.

oo^{n} pe^{n}t.

Eye-black. | O rimel.

oo ree′-mel.

Face-cream, face-cloth. | Creme, pano.

krem, pă′-noo.

Face powder. | Pó de arroz.

po dă-rosh′.

Fruit-salt. | Sal de fruta.

sal dĕ froo′-tă.

Gargle. | Um gargarejo.

oo^{n} găr-gă-ray′-zhoo.

English	Portuguese	Pronunciation
Hair-cream, hair-oil.	Brilhantina sólida, brilhantina líquida.	breel-ya^{n}-tee′-nă so′-lee-dă, breel-ya^{n}-tee′-nă lee′-kwee-dă.
Inhaler.	Um inalador.	oo^{n} ee-nă-lă-dohr′.
Jar (of face-cream etc.).	Um boião.	oo^{n} boh-yow^{n}′.
Lipstick, mirror.	O baton, espelho.	oo ba′-to^{n}, ish-payl′-yoo.
Make-up.	A maquilhagem.	a mă-keel-yah′-zhe^{n}.
Medicine.	Medicamento.	mĕ-dee-kă-me^{n}′-too.
Nail brush.	Escova de unhas.	ish-koh′-vă doon′-yăsh.
Nail file, nail varnish.	Lima de unhas, verniz de unhas.	lee′-mă doon′-yăsh, vĕr-neezh′ doon′-yăsh.
Nail varnish remover.	Acetona.	ă-sĕ-toh′-nă.
Ointment.	Unguento.	oo^{n}-gwe^{n}′-too.
Paper handkerchiefs.	Lenços de papel.	le^{n}′-soozh dĕ pă-pel′.
Pills, plaster.	Comprimidos, adesivo.	ko^{n}-prĕ-mee′-doosh, ă-dĕ-zee′-voo.
Pumice stone.	Uma pedra-pomes.	oo′-mă ped′-ră pomsh.
Quinine.	Quinino.	kĕ-nee′-noo.
Razor, blade.	Navalha de barba, lâmina.	nă-val′-yă dĕ bar′-bă, lă′-mee-nă.
Rouge.	O rouge.	oo roozh.

Sanitary towels.	Paninhos.
	pă-neen′-yoosh.
Scissors.	Tesouras.
	tĕ-zoh′-răsh.
Shaving brush, stick.	O pincel de barba, o estique de barbear.
	oo pee^{n}-sel′ dĕ bar′-bă, oo ish-teek′ dĕ băr-bee-ar′.
Shaving cream.	Creme para barbear.
	krem pă′-ră băr-bee-ar′.
Sleeping tablets.	Comprimidos para dormir.
	ko^{n}-prĕ-mee′-doosh pă′-ră door-meer′.
Sponge.	Esponja.
	ish-po^{n}′-zhă.
Stomach powder.	Pós digestivos.
	posh dee-zhĕsh-tee′-voosh.
Sunburn ointment.	Pomada para queimaduras do sol.
	poo-mah′-dă pă′-ră kay-ee-mă-doo′-răzh doo sol.
Sun glasses.	Óculos escuros.
	o′-koo-looz ish-koo′-roosh.
Sun tan lotion.	Loção de bronzear a pele.
	loh-sow^{n}′ dĕ bro^{n}-zee-ar′ ă pel.
Tooth brush.	Escova de dentes.
	ish-koh′-vă dĕ de^{n}tsh.
Tooth paste, powder.	Pasta de dentes, pós dentífricos.
	pash′-tă dĕ de^{n}tsh, pozh de^{n}-tee′-free-koosh.
Tube (of paste etc.)	Bisnaga.
	beezh-nah′-gă.

THE HAIRDRESSER

Can you recommend a hairdresser?	Pode recomendar-me um cabeleireiro?
	pod rĕ-koo-me^{n}-dar′-mee oo^{n} kă-bĕ-lay-ray′-ee-roo.

Can I make an appointment?	Posso marcar uma hora?

po′-soo măr-kar′ oo′-mă o′-ră.

When can I come?	Quando posso vir?

kwa^{n}′-doo po′-soo veer.

I want a haircut, a trim.	Desejo cortar o cabelo, espontar o cabelo.

dě-zay′-zhoo koor-tar′ oo kă-bay′-loo, ish-po^{n}-tar′ oo kă-bay′-loo.

Not too short.	Não muito curto.

now^{n} mwee^{n}′-too koor′-too.

Fairly short.	Um pouco curto.

oo^{n} poh′-koo koor′-too.

Don't take too much off the top.	Não corte muito em cima.

now^{n} kort mwee^{n}′-too e^{n} see′-mă.

Don't use the razor on the neck.	Não use a navalha no pescoço.

now^{n} ooz ă nă-val′-yă noo pěsh-koh′-soo.

At the back and sides.	Atrás e de lado.

ă-trash′ ee dě lah′-doo.

I want a shave.	Desejo fazer a barba.

dě-zay′-zhoo fă-zayr′ ă bar′-bă.

I want a shampoo.	Quero um shampoo.

kair′-oo oo^{n} sha^{n}-poo′.

The water is too hot, cold.	A água está muito quente, fria.

ag′-wă ish-ta′ mwee^{n}′-too ke^{n}t, free′-ă.

Shampoo and set.	Shampoo e mise-en-pli.

sha^{n}-poo′ ee meez-a^{n}-plee′.

I want my hair washed.	Desejo o cabelo lavado.

dě-zay′-zhoo oo kă-bay′-loo lă-vah′-doo.

I want a permanent wave.	Desejo uma permanente.

dě-zay′-zhoo oo′-mă pěr-mă-ne^{n}t′.

I part my hair on this side, in the middle. | Aparto o cabelo para este lado, ao meio.
ă-par′-too oo kă-bay′-loo pă′-ră aysht lah′-doo, ow may′-yoo.

I brush my hair straight back. | Aliso o cabelo para trás.
ă-lee′-zoo oo kă-bay′-loo pă′-ră trash.

Don't put anything on. | Não ponha nada nele.
now^{n} pohn′-yă nah′-dă nayl.

A little spray, cream. | Um borrifo, brilhantina.
oo^{n} boo-ree′-foo, breel-ya^{n}-tee′-nă.

Can I have a manicure? | Pode arranjar-me uma manicure?
pod ă-ra^{n}-zhar′-mee oo′-mă mă-nee-kyoor′.

Face massage. | Uma massagem da face.
oo′-mă mă-sah′-zhe^{n} dă fas.

To curl. | Frisar.
free-zar′.

Hair-pins, slide. | Ganchos de cabelo, travessa.
ga^{n}′-shoosh dĕ kă-bay′-loo, tră-ve′-să.

Hair-net, hair-oil. | Uma rede de cabelo, brilhantina.
oo′-mă rayd dĕ kă-bay′-loo, breel-ya^{n}-tee′-nă.

Dryer. | Um secador.
oo^{n} sĕ-kă-dohr′.

It is too hot. | Está muito quente.
ish-ta′ mwee^{n}′-too ke^{n}t.

PHOTOGRAPHY

Photography, photograph. | A fotografia.
ă foh-too-gră-fee′-ă.

Photographer. | O fotógrafo.
oo foh-to′-gră-foo.

I want some films for my camera. — Quero umas películas para a máquina.
kair′-oo oo′-măsh pĕ-lee′-koo-lăsh pă-rah′ ma′-kee-nă.

Have you colour films? — Tem películas a cores?
te^{n} pĕ-lee′-koo-laz ă koh′-rĕsh.

Can you develop these films? — Pode revelar estas películas?
pod rĕ-vĕ-lar′ esh′-tăsh pĕ-lee′-koo-lăsh.

One print of each. — Uma cópia de cada.
oo′-mă ko′-pee-ă dĕ kă′-dă.

When will they be ready? — Quando estarão prontas?
kwa^{n}′-doo ish-tă-row^{n}′ pro^{n}′-tăsh.

As soon as possible. — O mais depressa possível.
oo mȳzh dĕ-pre′-să poo-see′-vĕl.

Can you enlarge these snaps? — Pode ampliar estas fotos?
pod a^{n}-plee-ar′ esh′-tăsh foh′-toosh.

About this size. — Deste tamanho.
daysht tă-măn′-yoo.

My camera is broken. — A minha máquina partiu-se.
ă meen′-yă ma′-kee-nă păr-tee′-oos.

Can you adjust this camera? — Pode ajustar esta máquina?
pod ă-zhoosh-tar′ esh′-tă ma′-kee-nă.

This does not work properly. — Isto não funciona bem.
eesh′-too now^{n} foo^{n}-see-oh′-nă be^{n}.

How much will it cost? — Quanto custará?
kwa^{n}′-too koosh-tă-ra′.

BOOKSHOP AND STATIONER

I want to go to a bookshop (stationer's). — Quero ir a uma livraria (papelaria).
kair′-oo eer ă oo′-mă leev-ră-ree′-ă (pă-pĕ-lă-ree′-ă)

Have you any English books?	Tem livros ingleses?

ten leev′-rooz een-glayz′-ĕsh.

Have you any books by —— in English?	Tem livros de...em inglês?

ten leev′-roozh dĕ...en een-glaysh′.

I want an English-Portuguese dictionary.	Quero um dicionário inglês-português.

kair′-oo oon dee-see-oo-nah′-ree-oo een-glaysh′ poor-too-gaysh′.

Have you a book in very simple Portuguese?	Tem algum livro escrito em português muito simples?

ten al-goon′ leev′-roo ish-kree′-too en poor-too-gaysh′ mween′-too seen′-plĕsh.

Have you a map of the city, region, Portugal?	Tem um mapa da cidade, da região, de Portugal?

ten oon ma′-pă dă see-dahd′, dă rĕ-zhee-own′, dĕ poor-too-gal′.

I want some ink.	Quero tinta.

kair′-oo teen′-tă.

Writing-paper, envelopes.	Papel de escrever, envelopes.

pă-pel′ dish-krĕ-vayr′, en-vĕ-lopsh′.

Ball point pen.	Uma esferográfica.

oo′-mă ish-fe-roo-gra′-fee-kă.

Blotting paper.	Mataborrão.

ma-tă-boo-rown′.

Brown paper.	Papel de embrulhar.

pă-pel′ den-brool-yar′.

Brush.	Um pincel.

oon peen-sel′.

Fountain pen.	Uma caneta.

oo′-mă kă-nay′-tă.

Pen, nib.	Uma pena, um aparo.

oo′-mă pay′-nă, oon ă-pah′-roo.

Pencil, propelling-pencil. | Um lápis, uma lapiseira.

oo^{n} lahpsh, oo′-mă lă-pee-zay′-ee-ră.

Paper clips. | Clipes para papéis.

kleepsh pă′-ră pă-pe′-eesh.

Refill, rubber. | Recarga, borracha.

rĕ-kar′-gă, boo-rah′-shă.

Sealing-wax. | Lacre.

lakr.

THE BANK AND MONEY-CHANGERS

Banks in Portugal are generally open from 10 a.m. to mid-day and from 2 p.m. to 4 p.m. (Saturday, 10 a.m. to mid-day). Money-changers transact business generally from 9.30 a.m. to 6 p.m. and on Saturdays from 9.30 a.m. to 1 p.m.

Which is the way to the —— Bank? | Por onde se vai ao Banco ...?

poor o^{n}d sĕ vȳ ow ba^{n}′-koo...

Where are the money-changers? | Onde ficam as casas de câmbio?

o^{n}d fee′-kow^{n} ăsh kah′-zăzh dĕ ka^{n}′-bee-oo.

When do they open, close? | Quando abrem, fecham?

kwa^{n}-doo ab′-re^{n}, fay′-show^{n}.

I want to cash some traveller's cheques. | Quero descontar uns "traveller's cheques".

kair′-oo dĕsh-ko^{n}-tar′ oo^{n}sh "traveller's cheques".

Can you change this money, this note, for me? | Pode cambiar-me este dinheiro, esta nota?

pod ka^{n}-bee-ar′-mee aysht deen-yay′-ee-roo, esh′-tă no′-tă.

What is the rate of exchange? | Qual é o câmbio?

kwal e oo ka^{n}′-bee-oo.

I have a letter of credit. | Tenho uma carta de cré dito.

ten′-yoo oo′-mă kar′-tă dĕ kre′-dee-too.

I want to draw —— | Quero sacar um cheque de...
kair′-oo să-kar′ oo^{n} shek dĕ...

Here is my passport. | Aqui está o meu passaporte.
ă-kee′ ish-ta′ oo may′-oo pa-să-port′.

What is your address? | Qual é a sua morada?
kwal e ă soo′-ă moo-rah′-dă.

Do I sign here? | Devo assinar aqui?
day′-voo ă-see-nar′ ă-kee′.

May I see the manager? | Posso ver o gerente?
po′-soo vayr oo zhĕ-re^{n}t′.

May I speak to the cashier? | Posso falar com o caixa?
po′-soo fă-lar′ ko^{n} oo kȳ′-shă.

When shall I come back? | Quando devo voltar?
kwa^{n}′-doo day′-voo vohl-tar′.

I cannot wait so long. | Não posso esperar tanto tempo.
now^{n} po′-soo ish-pĕ-rar′ ta^{n}′-too te^{n}′-poo.

GENERAL SHOPPING VOCABULARY

Alarm clock. | Um despertador.
oo^{n} dish-pĕr-tă-dohr′.

Bathing cap, bathing costume. | Uma touca de borracha, um fato de banho.
oo′-mă toh′-kă dĕ boo-rah′-shă, oo^{n} fah′-too dĕ băn′-yoo.

Belt. | Um cinto.
oo^{n} see^{n}′-too.

Blouse. | Uma blusa.
oo′-mă bloo′-ză.

Bow-tie. | Um laço.
oo^{n} lah′-soo.

English	Portuguese	Pronunciation
Braces.	Suspensórios.	soosh-pe^{n}-so′-ree-oosh.
Button.	Um botão.	oo^{n} boo-tow^{n}′.
Camera.	Uma máquina fotográfica.	oo′-mă ma′-kee-nă foh-too-gra′-fee-kă.
Carpet.	Um tapete.	oo^{n} tă-payt′.
Clothes brush.	Uma escova de fato.	oo -mă ish-koh′-vă dĕ fah′-too.
Coat.	Um sobretudo.	oo^{n} soh-brĕ-too′-doo.
Coat-hanger.	Um cabide.	oo^{n} kă-beed′.
Collar.	Um colarinho.	oo^{n} koo-lă-reen′-yoo.
Comb.	Um pente.	oo^{n} pe^{n}t.
Cork.	Cortiça.	koor-tee′-să.
Cork (stopper for bottles)	Uma rolha.	oo′-mă rohl′-yă.
Cotton.	Algodão.	al-goo-dow^{n}′.
Cotton reel.	Um carro de linhas.	oo^{n} ka′-roo dĕ leen′-yăsh.
Cotton thread.	Linhas de passajar.	leen′-yăzh dĕ pă-să-zhar′.
Cuff links.	Botões de punho.	boo-toy^{n}zh′ dĕ poon′-yoo.
Dress.	Um vestido.	oo^{n} vĕsh-tee′-doo.
Dressing gown.	Um robe.	oo^{n} rob.

Dress material. | Tecido para vestidos.
tě-see′-doo pă′-ră věsh-tee′-doosh.

Embroidery work. | Bordados.
boor-dah′-doosh.

Evening dress (men). | Um fato de cerimónia.
oo^n fah′-too dě sě-rě-mo′-nee-ă.

Evening dress (women). | Um vestido de noite.
oo^n věsh-tee′-doo dě noh′-eet.

Filigree-work. | Filigrana.
fě-lee-gră′-nă.

Garters. | Ligas.
lee′-găsh.

Gloves. | Luvas.
loo′-văsh.

Gramophone record. | Um disco.
oo^n deesh′-koo.

Hair brush. | Uma escova de cabelo.
oo′-mă ish-koh′-vă dě kă-bay′-loo.

Handbag. | Uma carteira.
oo′-mă kăr-tay′-ee-ră.

Handkerchief. | Um lenço.
oo^n le^n′-soo.

Hat. | Um chapéu.
oo^n shă-pe′-oo.

Head scarf. | Um lenço de cabeça.
oo^n le^n′-soo dě kă-bay′-să.

Jacket. | Um casaco.
oo^n kă-zah′-koo.

Lipstick. | Um baton.
oo^n ba′-to^n.

Magazine. | Uma revista.
oo′-mă rě-veesh′-tă.

Mat. | Uma esteira.
oo′-mă ish-tay′-ee-ră.

English	Portuguese	Pronunciation
Mirror.	Um espelho.	oo^{n} ish-payl′-yoo.
Needle.	Uma agulha.	oo′-mă ă-gool′-yă.
Newspaper.	Um jornal.	oo^{n} zhoor-nal′.
Nightdress.	Uma camisa de dormir.	oo′-mă kă-mee′-ză dĕ door-meer′.
Pants.	Cuecas.	koo-e′-kăsh.
Pins.	Alfinetes.	al-fee-netsh′.
Pottery.	Louça.	loh′-să.
Pullover.	Um pullover.	oo^{n} poo-loh′-ver.
Purse.	Uma porta-moedas.	oo′-mă por′-tă moo-e′-dăsh.
Pyjamas.	Pijamas.	pee-zhă′-măsh.
Raincoat.	Um impermeável.	oo^{n} ee^{n}-pĕr-mee-ah′-vĕl.
Rouge.	Rouge.	roozh.
Rug (travelling), rug (floor).	Manta de viagem, um tapete.	ma^{n}′-tă dĕ vee-ah′-zhe^{n}, oo^{n} tă-payt′.
Safety pins.	Alfinetes de segurança.	al-fee-netsh′ dĕ sĕ-goo-ra^{n}′-să.
Scarf (men).	Um cachecol.	oo^{n} kash-kol′.
Scarf (women).	Um lenço de pescoço.	oo^{n} le^{n}′-soo dĕ pĕsh-koh′-soo.
Shirt.	Uma camisa.	oo′-ma kă-mee′-ză.

Shoes.	Sapatos.
să-pah′-toosh.	
Shoe brush.	Uma escova de calçado.
oo′-mă ish-koh′-vă dĕ kal-sah′-doo.	
Shoe laces.	Atacadores de sapatos.
ă-tă-kă-doh′-rĕzh dĕ să-pah′-toosh.	
Shoe polish.	Graxa; pomada para calçado.
gra′-shă; poo-mah′-dă pă′-ră kal-sah′-doo.	
Shop.	Loja.
lo′-zhă.	
Silk.	Seda.
say′-dă.	
Skirt.	Uma saia.
oo′-mă sȳ′-yă.	
Slippers.	Chinelas.
shee-ne′-lăsh.	
Socks.	Peugas.
pee-oo′-găsh.	
Souvenir gifts.	Lembranças.
le^{n}-bra^{n}′-săsh.	
Stamps.	Selos.
say′-loosh.	
Stockings.	Meias.
may′-yăsh.	
Studs.	Botões de colarinho.
boo-toy^{n}zh′ dĕ koo-lă-reen′-yoo.	
Suit.	Um fato.
oo^{n} fah′-too.	
Suit-case.	Uma mala.
oo′-mă ma′-lă.	
Sun-glasses.	Óculos escuros.
o′-koo-looz ish-koo′-roosh.	
Suspenders.	Ligas.
lee′-găsh.	

Swim-suit.	Um fato de banho.
oo^{n} fah'-too dĕ băn'-yoo.	
Tie.	Uma gravata.
oo'-mă gră-vah'-tă.	
Tiles (glazed, for decoration).	Azulejos.
ă-zoo-lay'-zhoosh.	
Towel.	Uma toalha.
oo'-mă too-al'-yă.	
Toys.	Brinquedos.
bree^{n}-kay'-doosh.	
Travelling rug.	Uma manta de viagem.
oo'-mă ma^{n}'-tă dĕ vee-ah'-zhe^{n}.	
Trousers.	Calças.
kal'-săsh.	
Umbrella.	Um guarda-chuva.
oo^{n} gwar'-dă shoo'-vă.	
Underclothes.	Roupa interior.
roh'-pă ee^{n}-tĕ-ree-ohr'.	
Waistcoat.	Um colete.
oo^{n} koo-layt'.	
Walking-stick.	Uma bengala.
oo'-mă be^{n}-ga'-lă.	
Wallet.	Uma carteira.
oo'-mă kăr-tay'-ee-ră.	
Watch.	Um relógio.
oo^{n} rĕ-lo'-zhee-oo.	
Zip-fastener.	Um fecho de correr
oo^{n} fay'-shoo dĕ koo-rayr'.	

This is not my size.	Não é a minha medida.
now^{n} e ă meen'-yă mĕ-dee'-dă.	
It is too big, small.	É muito grande, pequeno
e mwee^{n}'-too gra^{n}d, pĕ-kay'-noo.	

It is too wide, narrow, tight. | É muito largo, estreito, apertado.
e mwee^n′-too lar′-goo, ish-tray′-ee-too, ă-pĕr-tah′-doo.

It is too long, short. | É muito comprido, curto.
e mwee^n′-too ko^n-pree′-doo, koor′-too.

This is not what I want. | Isto não é o que desejo.
eesh′-too now^n e oo kĕ dĕ-zay′-zhoo.

I do not like this. | Não gosto disto.
now^n gohsh′-too deesh′-too.

I can't see the colour clearly here. | Não vejo bem a cor aqui.
now^n vay′-zhoo be^n ă kohr ă-kee′.

I do not like the colour, pattern. | Não gosto da cor, do desenho.
now^n gohsh′-too dă kohr, doo dĕ-zayn′-yoo.

It is too dark, light. | É muito escuro, claro.
e mwee^n′-too ish-koo′-roo, klah′-roo.

Colour. | A cor.
ă kohr.

Black, white, red. | Preto, branco, vermelho.
pray′-too, bra^n′-koo, vĕr-may′-lyoo.

Green, grey, brown. | Verde, cinzento, castanho.
verd, see^n-ze^n′-too, kăsh-tăn′-yoo.

Blue, light blue, dark blue. | Azul, azul claro, azul escuro.
ă-zool′, ă-zool′ klah′-roo, ă-zool′ ish-koo′-roo.

Yellow, pink. | Amarelo, côr de rosa.
ă-mă-ray′-loo, kohr dĕ ro′-ză.

I want a better quality. | Quero uma qualidade melhor.
kair′-oo oo′-mă kwa-lee-dahd′ mĕl-yor′.

I want something simple, plain. | Quero uma coisa simples.
kair′-oo oo′-mă koh′-ee-ză see^n′-plĕsh.

I want something cheaper, dearer.	Quero uma coisa mais barata, mais cara.
kair′-oo oo′-mă koh′-ee-ză mȳzh bă-rah′-tă, mȳzh kah′-ră.	
Does this material shrink?	Esta fazenda encolhe?
esh′-tă fă-ze^{n}′-dă e^{n}-kol′-yĕ.	
May I try this on?	Posso prová-lo?
po′-soo proo-va′-loo.	
May I see how it looks in the mirror?	Posso ver como é ao espelho?
po′-soo vayr koh′-moo e ow ish-payl′-yoo.	
It does not fit me.	Não me assenta bem.
now^{n} mee ă-se^{n}′-tă be^{n}.	
It does not fit here.	Não assenta bem aqui.
now^{n} ă-se^{n}′-tă be^{n} ă-kee′.	
It does not suit me.	Não me convém.
now^{n} mĕ ko^{n}-ve^{n}′.	
Have you nothing else, nothing better?	Não tem outra coisa, outra coisa melhor?
now^{n} te^{n} oh′-tră koh′-ee-ză, oh′-tră koh′-ee-ză mĕl-yor′.	
What is the charge for making one?	Quanto custa para fazer um?
kwa^{n}′-too koosh′-tă pă′-ră fă-zayr′ oo^{n}.	
When could it be ready?	Quando estaria pronto?
kwa^{n}′-doo ish-tă-ree′-ă pro^{n}′-too.	
Please send it.	Faz favor de mandá-lo.
fash fă-vohr′ dĕ ma^{n}-da′-loo.	
I will take it with me.	Levo-o comigo.
le′-voo-oo koo-mee′-goo.	
I shall pay on delivery.	Pagarei na entrega.
pă-gă-ray′-ee nă e^{n}-tre′-gă.	
I have not enough money with me.	Não tenho bastante dinheiro aqui.
now^{n} ten′-yoo băsh-ta^{n}t′ deen-yay′-ee-roo ă-kee′.	

I shall come back for it. | Volto por ele.
vol′-too poor ayl.

Please reserve it. | Faz favor de reservá-lo.
fash fă-vohr′ dĕ rĕ-zĕr-va′-loo.

I must have it before —— | Preciso disto antes de...
prĕ-see′-zoo deesh′-too a^{n}tsh dĕ...

I am leaving tomorrow. | Parto amanhã.
par′-too a-măn-ya^{n}′.

Don't forget. | Não se esqueça.
now^{n} see ish-ke′-să.

REPAIRS

I want to take these shoes to a shoemaker's. | Quero levar estes sapatos a um sapateiro.
kair′-oo lĕ-var′ ayshtsh să-pah′-toosh ă oo^{n} să-pă-tay′-ee-roo.

Soles, heels (men); heels (women). | Solas, tacões; saltos.
so′-lăsh, tă-koy^{n}sh′; sal′-toosh.

Rubber. | Borracha.
boo-rah′-shă.

This needs mending. | Isto precisa de ser consertado.
eesh′-too prĕ-see′-ză dĕ sayr ko^{n}-sĕr-tah′-doo.

Can you mend this? | Pode consertar-me isto?
pod ko^{n}-sĕr-tar′-mĕ eesh′-too.

When will it be ready? | Quando estará pronto?
kwa^{n}′-doo ish-tă-ra′ pro^{n}′-too.

These spectacles need repairing. | Estes óculos precisam de ser consertados.
ayshtz o′-koo-loosh prĕ-see′-zow^{n} dĕ sayr ko^{n}-sĕr-tah′-doosh.

They are damaged here. | Estão estragados aqui.
ish-tow^{n}′ ish-tră-gah′-dooz ă-kee′.

I need a new lens, frame.	Preciso de uma lente nova, armação nova.
pre-see′-zoo doom′-ă le^{n}t no′-vă, ăr-mă-sow^{n}′ no′-vă.	
I want a new case.	Quero um estojo novo.
kair′-oo oo^{n} ish-toh′-zhoo noh′-voo.	
Too tight, slack.	Muito apertado, largo.
mwee^{n}′-too ă-pĕr-tah′-doo, lar′-goo.	
The spectacles are not straight.	Os óculos não estão direitos.
ooz o′-koo-loozh now^{n} ish-tow^{n}′ dee-ray′-ee-toosh.	
I want some dark glasses to fit on these.	Quero óculos escuros para adaptar nestes.
kair′-oo o′-koo-looz ish-koo′-roosh pă′-ră ă-dap-tar′ nayshtsh.	
My watch has stopped.	O meu relógio parou.
oo may′-oo rĕ-lo′-zhee-oo pă-roh′.	
My watch is broken.	O meu relógio está partido.
oo may′-oo rĕ-lo′-zhee-oo ish-ta′ păr-tee′-doo.	
The glass is broken.	O vidro está partido.
oo veed′-roo ish-ta′ păr-tee′-doo.	
The watch needs cleaning.	O relógio precisa de limpeza.
oo rĕ-lo′-zhee-oo prĕ-see′-ză dĕ lee^{n}-pay′-ză.	
It gains, loses.	Adianta, atrasa.
ă-dee-a^{n}′-tă, ă-trah′-ză.	
Can you regulate it?	Pode acertá-lo?
pod ă-sĕr-ta′-loo.	
I overwound it.	Dei-lhe muita corda.
day′-ee-lyĕ mwee^{n}′-tă kor′-dă.	
I dropped it.	Deixei-o cair.
day-ee-shay′-yoo kă-eer′.	
A new strap.	Uma correia nova.
oo′-mă koo-ray′-yă no′-vă.	

Can you repair this camera?	Pode reparar esta máquina?

pod rĕ-pă-rar′ esh′-tă ma′-kee-nă.

This does not work.	Isto não funciona.

eesh′-too now^{n} foon-see-oh′-nă.

I can't wind the film.	Não posso enrolar a película.

now^{n} po′-soo e^{n}-roo-lar′ ă pĕ-lee′-koo-lă.

The lock on this case won't work.	A fechadura desta mala não funciona.

ă fĕ-shă-doo′-ră desh′-tă ma′-lă now^{n} foon-see-oh′-nă.

I need a new handle.	Preciso de uma pegadeira nova.

prĕ-see′-zoo doo′-mă pĕ-gă-day′-ee-ră no′-vă.

How long will it take?	Quanto tempo leva?

kwa^{n}′-too te^{n}-poo le′-vă.

When can I come for it?	Quando posso vir por ela?

kwa^{n}′-doo po′-soo veer poor e′-lă.

I want these stockings, socks.	Desejo estas meias, peugas, consertadas

dĕ-zay′-zhoo esh′-tăzh may′-yăsh, pee-oo′-găsh, ko^{n}-sĕr-tah′-dăsh.

Can you sew, stitch, this?	Pode coser isto?

pod koo-zayr′ eesh′-too.

POLICE

Travellers are required to register with the police on arrival at hotel or boarding-house. The registration form is provided by the management, who usually arrange for it to be sent to the police.

Lists of lost property handed in to the police generally appear in the daily papers.

I want to speak to a policeman.	Quero falar com um polícia.
kair′-oo fă-lar′ ko^{n} oo^{n} poo-lee′-see-ă.	
Where is the police-station?	Onde é a polícia?
o^{n}d′-ee e ă poo-lee′-see-ă	
I wish to register as a foreign visitor, business man.	Quero registar-me como turista estrangeiro, comerciante estrangeiro.
kair′-oo rĕ-zheesh-tar′-mĕ koh′-moo too-reesh′-tă ish-tra^{n}-zhay′-ee-roo, koo-mĕr-see-a^{n}t′ ish-tra^{n}-zhay′-ee-roo.	
I am British.	Sou inglês.
soh ee^{n}-glaysh′.	
I am a British citizen.	Sou cidadão britânico.
soh see-dă-dow^{n}′ bree-tă′-nee-koo.	
I am staying at ——	Moro em...
mo′-roo e^{n}...	
I intend staying here for ——	Tenciono demorar-me aqui...
te^{n}-see-oh′-noo dĕ-moo-rar′-mee ă-kee′...	
Have I to inform you when I am leaving?	Tenho de os informar quando partir?
ten′-yoo dee ooz ee^{n}-foor-mar′ kwa^{n}′-doo păr-teer′.	
I have my passport.	Tenho o meu passaporte.
ten′-yoo oo may′-oo pa-să-port′.	

I have lost ——	Perdi...
pĕr-dee′...	
Is it worth advertising?	Vale a pena anunciá-lo no jornal?
val ă pay′-nă ă-noo^n-see-a′-loo noo zhoor-nal′.	
Will you inform me if it is found?	Poderá informar-me se for achado?
poo-dĕ-ra′ ee^n-foor-mar′-mĕ sĕ fohr ă-shah′-doo.	
I shall offer a reward.	Ofereço uma recompensa.
oh-fray′-soo oo′-mă rĕ-ko^n-pe^n′-să.	
Shall I call tomorrow?	Posso vir cá amanhã?
po′-soo veer ka a-măn-ya^n′.	

ACCIDENTS

Help! | Socorro!
soo-koh′-roo.

Quickly! | Depressa!
dĕ-pre′-să.

Come here! | Venha cá.
ven′-yă ka.

There has been an accident. | Houve um acidente.
ohv oo^{n} ă-see-de^{n}t′.

Bring a doctor, policeman. | Chame um médico, um polícia.
sham oo^{n} me′-dee-koo, oo^{n} poo-lee′-see-ă.

Ambulance, nurse. | Ambulância, uma enfermeira.
a^{n}-boo-la^{n}′-see-ă, oo′-mă e^{n}-fĕr-may′-ee-ră.

Hurt, injured. | Magoado, ferido.
mă-gwah′-doo, fĕ-ree′-doo.

I am all right. | Estou bem.
ish-toh′ be^{n}.

Are you all right? | Está bem?
ish-ta′ be^{n}.

It was (not) my fault. | A culpa (não) foi minha.
ă kool′-pă (now^{n}) foh′-ee meen′-yă.

He did not see (hear) me. | Não me viu (ouviu).
now^{n} mĕ vee′-oo (oh-vee′-oo).

I don't understand. | Não percebo.
now^{n} pĕr-say′-boo.

Does anyone speak English? | Alguém fala inglês?
al-ge^{n}′ fa′-lă ee^{n}-glaysh′.

I feel better now. | Já estou melhor.
zha ish-toh′ mĕl-yor′.

I don't think it's serious. | Não creio que seja grave.
now^{n} kray′-yoo kĕ say′-zhă grahv.

I just want to sit down a while. | Só quero sentar-me um pouco.
so kair′-oo se^{n}-tar′-mĕ oo^{n} poh′-koo.

Where is the nearest doctor, chemist? | Onde está o médico mais próximo, farmácia mais próxima?
o^{n}d ish-ta′ oo me′-dee-koo mȳsh pro′-see-moo, făr-mah′-see-ă mȳsh pro′-see-mă.

First-aid post. | O posto de socorros.
oo pohsh′-too dĕ soo-koh′-roosh.

I am hurt here. | Estou magoado aqui.
ish-toh′ mă-gwah′-doo ă-kee′.

I can't move. | Não posso mover-me.
now^{n} po′-soo moo-vayr′-mĕ.

It hurts me to move. | Dói quando me mexo.
doy kwa^{n}′-doo mĕ me′-shoo.

The pain is here. | Dói-me aqui.
doy′-mee ă-kee′.

There is a cut here. | Há um corte aqui.
ah oo^{n} kort ă-kee′.

I feel faint. | Sinto desmaiar-me.
see^{n}′-too dĕzh-mȳ-yar′-mĕ.

Can you bandage this? | Pode ligar isto?
pod lee-gar′ eesh′-too.

Press here! | Aperte aqui!
ă-pairt′ ă-kee′.

That hurts. | Isso dói.
ee′-soo doy.

Gently, hard. | Com jeito, firme.
ko^{n} zhay′-ee-too, feerm.

Someone is drowning.	Uma pessoa está a afogar-se.

oo′-mă pĕ-soh′-ă ish-ta′ ă-foo-gars′.

THE DENTIST

I want to go to a good dentist.	Quero ir a um dentista bom.

kair′-oo eer ă oo^{n} de^{n}-teesh′-tă bo^{n}.

I have toothache.	Tenho dor de dentes.

ten′-yoo dohr dĕ de^{n}tsh.

I have lost a filling.	Perdi uma obturação.

pĕr-dee′ oo′-mă ob-too-ră-sow^{n}′.

A tooth is broken.	Um dente partiu-se.

oo^{n} de^{n}t păr-tee′-oos.

I can't see signs of decay.	Não vejo sinais de deterioração.

now^{n} vay′-zhoo see-nÿzh′ dĕ dĕ-tĕ-ree-oo-ră-sow^{n}′.

Must it come out?	É preciso tirá-lo?

e prĕ-see′-zoo tee-ra′-loo.

That hurts.	Isso dói.

ee′-soo doy.

Can I have a temporary filling?	Pode fazer-me uma obturação provisória?

pod fă-zayr′-mee oo′-mă ob-too-ră-sow^{n}′ proo-vee-zo′-ree-ă.

How long will it take?	Quanto tempo levará?

kwa^{n}′-too te^{n}′-poo lĕ-vă-ra′.

I leave on ——	Parto...

par′-too...

The gum is bleeding.	A gengiva está a sangrar

ă zhe^{n}-zhee′-vă ish-ta′ ă sa^{n}-grar′.

The gum is sore.	A gengiva está dorida.

ă zhe^{n}-zhee′-vă ish-ta′ doo-ree′-dă.

That is much better.	Isso é muito melhor.

ee′-soo e mwee^{n}′-too mĕl-yor′.

How much do I owe you? | Quanto lhe devo?
kwa^{n}-too lyĕ day′-voo′.

Gas. | Gás.
gash.

Gold, ordinary filling. | Obturação de ouro, normal.
ob-too-ră-sow^{n}′ doh′-roo, nohr-mal′.

These false teeth are broken. | Esta dentadura partiu-se.
esh-tă de^{n}-tă-doo′-ră păr-tee′-oos.

THE DOCTOR

I must see a doctor. | Tenho de ir a um médico.
ten′-yoo dĕ eer ă oo^{n} me′-dee-koo.

Please call a doctor. | Faz favor de chamar um médico.
fash fă-vohr′ dĕ shă-mar′ oo^{n} me′-dee-koo.

I don't feel well. | Não me sinto bem.
now^{n} mĕ see^{n}′-too be^{n}.

I feel feverish. | Sinto-me febril.
see^{n}′-too-mĕ fĕ-breel′.

I feel very weak. | Sinto-me muito fraco.
see^{n}′-too-mĕ mwee^{n}′-too frah′-koo.

I have a headache. | Tenho dor de cabeça.
ten′-yoo dohr dĕ kă-bay′-să.

Sore throat. | Dor de garganta.
dohr dĕ găr-ga^{n}′-tă.

Ear-ache, tooth-ache. | Dor de ouvidos, dor de dentes.
dohr doh-vee′-doosh, dohr dĕ de^{n}tsh.

I have a persistent cough. | Tenho uma tosse constante.
ten′-yoo oo′-mă tos ko^{n}sh-ta^{n}t′.

I have an infection in ——	Tenho uma infecção em . . .
ten′-yoo oo′-mă ee^{n}-fe-sow^{n}′ e^{n}. . .	
I have hurt my hand, finger, arm.	Magoei-me na mão, no dedo, no braço.
mă-goo-ay′-ee-mĕ nă mow^{n}, noo day′-doo, noo brah′-soo.	
Leg, foot, shoulder.	Perna, pé, ombro.
pair′-nă, pe, o^{n}′-broo.	
I am (temporarily) deaf.	Estou surdo.
ish-toh′ soor′-doo.	
Perhaps the ear needs syringing.	Talvez o ouvido precise de limpeza.
tal-vayz′ oo oh-vee′-doo prĕ-seez′ dĕ lee^{n}-pay′-ză.	
I have a rash.	Tenho urticária.
ten′-yoo oor-tee-kah′-ree-ă.	
I have a splinter in my finger.	Tenho uma farpa de madeira no dedo.
ten′-yoo oo′-mă far′-pă dĕ mă-day′-ee-ră noo day′-doo.	
Take this medicine with water three times a day	Tome este medicamento com água três vezes por dia.
tom aysht mĕ-dee-kă-me^{n}′-too ko^{n} ag′-wă trayzh vay′-zĕsh poor dee′-ă.	
Before, after, meals.	Antes de, depois de, comer.
a^{n}tsh dĕ, dĕ-poh′-eezh dĕ, koo-mayr′.	
Take this note to the hospital.	Leve esta nota para o hospital.
lev esh′-tă no′-tă pă′-ră oo osh-pee-tal′.	
Must I stay in bed?	Devo ficar na cama?
day′-voo fee-kar′ nă kă′-mă.	
Can I eat anything?	Posso comer qualquer coisa?
po′-soo koo-mayr′ kwal′-kair koh′-ee-ză.	

Should I come back?	Devo voltar amanhã?

day'-voo vohl-tar' a-măn-ya^{n}'.

Will you visit me tomorrow?	Pode visitar-me amanhã?

pod vě-zee-tar'-mee a-măn-ya^{n}'.

AT TABLE

Where is the restaurant, dining-room?	Onde é o restaurante, a sala de jantar?
o^{n}d′-ee e oo rĕsh-tow-ra^{n}t′, ă sa′-la dĕ zha^{n}-tar′.	
When is lunch, dinner, served?	A que horas é o almoço, o jantar?
ă kee o′-răz e oo al-moh′-soo, oo zha^{n}-tar′.	
The head waiter.	O chefe de serviço.
oo shef dĕ sĕr-vee′-soo.	
The waiter.	O criado.
oo kree-ah′-doo.	
A table for two.	Uma mesa para dois.
oo′-mă may′-ză pă′-ră doh′-eesh.	
Where can we sit?	Onde podemos sentar-nos?
o^{n}d poo-day′-moosh se^{n}-tar′-noosh.	
A table by the window, the wall.	Uma mesa perto da janela, junto da parede.
oo′-mă may′-ză pair′-too dă zhă-ne′-lă, zhoo^{n}′-too dă pă-rayd′.	
There is a draught here.	Há uma corrente de ar aqui.
ah oo′-mă koo-re^{n}t′ dar ă-kee′.	
Are you being served?	Está servido?
ish-ta′ sĕr-vee′-doo.	
May we have the menu?	A ementa (a lista, o menú), se faz favor.
ă ee-me^{n}′-tă (ă leesh′-tă, oo mĕn-yoo′), sĕ fash fă-vohr′.	
We should like ——	Queríamos...
kĕ-ree′-ă-moosh...	
Bring ——	Traga...
trah′-gă...	

What do you recommend?	Que recomenda?
	kĕ rĕ-koo-me^{n}′-dă.
What is this?	O que é isto?
	oo kee e eesh′-too.
What is this in English?	O que é isto em inglês?
	oo kee e eesh′-too e^{n} ee^{n}-glaysh′.
Is it good?	É bom?
	e bo^{n}.
I don't want anything greasy.	Não quero coisas gordurosas.
	now^{n} kair′-oo koh′-ee-zăzh goor-doo-ro′-zăsh.
I don't like a lot of olive oil.	Não gosto de muito azeite.
	now^{n} gohsh′-too dĕ mwee^{n}′-too ă-zay′-eet.
I don't like garlic.	Não gosto de alho.
	now^{n} gohsh′-too dal′-yoo.
I don't like this.	Não gosto disto.
	now^{n} gohsh′-too deesh′-too.
Take this away.	Pode levar isto daqui.
	pod lĕ-var′ eesh′-too dă-kee′.
Can I have something else?	Posso comer outra coisa?
	po′-soo koo-mayr′ oh′-tră koh′-ee-ză.
This is not clean.	Isto não está limpo.
	eesh′-too now^{n} ish-ta′ lee^{n}′-poo.
Bring me another spoon, knife, fork.	Traga outra colher, faca, outro garfo.
	trah′-gă oh′-tră kool-yair′, fah′-kă, oh′-troo gar′-foo.
Napkin.	Um guardanapo.
	oo^{n} gwar-dă-nah′-poo.
Would you like some more?	Deseja mais?
	dĕ-zay′-zhą̆ mȳsh.

Would you like some other dish? | Deseja outro prato?

dě-zay′-zhă oh′-troo prah′-too.

Would you like something more? | Deseja mais alguma coisa?

dě-zay′-zhă mȳz al-goo′-mă koh′-ee-ză.

No, thank you, I have had sufficient. | Obrigado, não desejo mais.

oh-bree-gah′-doo, now^{n} dě-zay′-zhoo mȳsh.

Yes, please. | Sim, faz favor.

see^{n}, fash fă-vohr′.

Bring the bill, please. | Dê-me a conta, se faz favor.

day′-mee ă ko^{n}′-tă, sě fash fă-vohr′.

Is the service included? | O serviço está incluido?

oo sěr-vee′-soo ish-ta′ ee^{n}-kloo-ee′-doo.

The bill is not correct. | A conta não está certa.

ă ko^{n}′-tă now^{n} ish-ta′ sair′-tă.

I shall pay for all of us. | Eu pago por todos.

ay′-oo pah′-goo poor toh′-doosh.

We shall pay separately. | Pagamos separadamente.

pă-gă′-moosh sě-pă-rah′-dă-me^{n}t.

MENU AND UTENSILS

Almonds. | Amêndoas.

ă-me^{n}′-doo-ăsh.

Apples. | Maçãs.

mă-sa^{n}sh′.

Apricots. | Damascos

dă-mash′-koosh.

Asparagus. | Espargo.

ish-par′-goo.

Bananas. | Bananas.

bă-nă′-năsh.

English	Portuguese	Pronunciation
Beans (broad).	Favas.	fah′-văsh.
Beans (haricot).	Feijão verde.	fay-ee-zhow^n′ verd.
Beef (boiled).	Carne cozida.	karn koo-zee′-dă.
Beef (roast).	Carne assada.	karn ă-sah′-dă.
Beef-steak.	Um bife.	oo^n beef.
Beer.	Cerveja.	sĕr-vay′-zhă.
Biscuit.	Bolacha.	boo-lah′-shă.
Boiled.	Cozido.	koo-zee′-doo.
Bottle, large bottle.	Garrafa, um garrafão.	gă-rah′-fă, oo^n gă-ră-fow^n′.
Brandy.	O brandy; brande.	oo bra^n′-dee.
Bread.	O pão.	oo pow^n.
Butter.	Manteiga.	ma^n-tay′-ee-gă.
Cabbage, cabbage-soup.	A couve, caldo verde.	ă kohv, kal′-doo verd.
Cake.	Bolo.	boh′-loo.
Carrots.	Cenouras.	sĕ-noh′-răsh.
Cauliflower.	A couve-flor.	ă koh′-vĕ-flohr.
Cheese.	Queijo.	kay′-ee-zhoo.

Chicken, chicken-soup. | Frango, canja.
fra^{n}′-goo, ka^{n}′-zhă.

Chocolate. | O chocolate.
oo shoo-koo-laht′.

Chop (mutton, pork). | Costeleta (de carneiro, de porco).
koosh-tĕ-lay′-ta (dĕ kăr-nay′-ee-roo, dĕ pohr′-koo).

Cockles. | Amêijoas.
ă-may′-ee-zhoo-ăsh.

Cod. | O bacalhau.
oo bă-kăl-yow′.

Coffee. | O café.
oo kă-fe′.

Cold meat. | Carne fria.
karn free′-ă.

Crab. | Caranguejo.
kă-ra^{n}-gay′-zhoo.

Cream. | Nata.
nah′-tă.

Cucumber. | Pepino.
pĕ-pee′-noo.

Cup. | Chávena.
shah′-vĕ-nă.

Dates. | Tâmaras.
tă′-mă-răsh.

Dessert. | A sobremesa.
ă soh-brĕ-may′-ză.

Dinner. | O jantar.
oo zha^{n}-tar′.

Duck. | Pato.
pah′-too.

Eel. | Enguia.
e^{n}-gee′-ă.

Egg, eggs. | Ovo, ovos.
oh′-voo, o′-voosh.

Egg, soft boiled, hard boiled.	Ovo, mal cozido, ovo cozido.
oh′-voo, mal koo-zee′-doo, oh′-voo koo-zee′-doo.	
Eggs, fried, poached.	Ovo, estrelado, escalfado.
oh′-voo, ish-trĕ-lah′-doo, ish-kal-fah′-doo.	
Figs.	Figos.
fee′-goosh.	
Fish.	O peixe.
oo pay′-eesh.	
Fish, fried, boiled.	Peixe, frito, cozido.
pay′-eesh, free′-too, koo-zee′-doo.	
Fork.	Garfo.
gar′-foo.	
Fried.	Frito.
free′-too.	
Fruit.	Fruta.
froo′-tă.	
Fruit pie.	Empada de fruta.
e^{n}-pah′-dă dĕ froo′-tă.	
Fruit tart.	Torta de fruta.
tor′-tă dĕ froo′-tă.	
Garlic.	Alho.
al′-yoo.	
Gin	Genebra.
zhĕ-ne′-bră.	
Glass.	Copo.
ko′-poo.	
Grapes.	Uvas.
oo′-văsh.	
Gravy.	Molho.
mohl′-yoo.	
Grilled.	Grelhado.
grĕl-yah′-doo.	
Hake.	Pescada.
pĕsh-kah′-dă.	

Ham. | O fiambre.
oo fee-a^{n}br′.

Ham, smoked. | Presunto.
prĕ-zoo^{n}′-too.

Herring. | O arenque.
oo ă-re^{n}k′.

Hors d'œuvres. | O hors d'œuvres, acepipes variados.
oo "hors d'œuvres", ă-sĕ-peepsh′ vă-ree-ah′-doosh.

Ice. | Gelo.
zhay′-loo.

Ice-cream. | Gelado.
zhĕ-lah′-doo.

Jam. | Compota de fruta.
ko^{n}-po′-tă dĕ froo′-tă.

Jam (quince). | Marmelada.
măr-mĕ-lah′-dă.

Juice, orange, grape, tomato. | Sumo de laranja, de uva, de tomate.
soo′-moo dĕ lă-ra^{n}′-zhă, doo′-vă, dĕ too-maht′.

Kidney. | O rim.
oo ree^{n}.

Knife. | Faca.
fah′-kă.

Lamb. | Cordeiro, borrego.
koor-day′-ee-roo, boo-ray′-goo.

Lemon. | Um limão.
oo^{n} lee-mow^{n}′.

Lemonade. | Limonada.
lee-moo-nah′-dă.

Lettuce. | A alface.
ă al-fas′.

Liqueur. | O licor
oo lee-kohr′.

English	Portuguese	Pronunciation
Liver.	Fígado.	fee′-gă-doo.
Lobster.	Lagosta.	lă-gohsh′-tă.
Lunch.	Almoço.	al-moh′-soo.
Marmalade.	Compota de laranja.	ko^{n}-po′-tă dĕ lă-ra^{n}′-zhă.
Marrow.	Abóbora.	ă-bo′-boo-ră.
Meat.	A carne.	ă karn.
Melon, water melon.	Um melão, melancia.	oo^{n} mĕ-low^{n}′, mĕ-la^{n}-see′-ă.
Milk.	O leite.	oo lay′-eet.
Mineral water.	Água mineral.	ag′-wă mee-nĕ-ral′.
Mushrooms.	Cogumelos.	koh-goo-me′-loosh.
Mustard.	Mostarda.	moosh-tar′-dă.
Mutton.	Carneiro.	kăr-nay′-ee-roo.
Napkin.	Guardanapo.	gwar-dă-nah′-poo.
Nuts.	Nozes.	no′-zĕsh.
Octopus.	Polvo.	pohl′-voo.
Olive-oil.	O azeite.	oo ă-zay′-eet.
Olives.	Azeitonas.	ă-zay-ee-toh′-năsh.

English	Portuguese	Pronunciation
Omelette.	Omeleta.	ohm-lay′-tă.
Onion.	Cebola.	sĕ-boh′-lă.
Orange.	Laranja.	lă-ra^{n}′-zhă.
Oysters.	Ostras.	osh′-trăsh.
Peach.	Pêssego.	pay′-sĕ-goo.
Pear.	Pera.	pay′-ră.
Peas.	Ervilhas.	ĕr-veel′-yăsh.
Pepper.	Pimenta.	pee-me^{n}′-tă.
Pheasant, partridge.	O faisão, perdiz.	oo fă-ee-zow^{n}′, pĕr-deesh′.
Pineapple.	O ananás.	oo ă-nă-nash′.
Plate.	Prato.	prah′-too.
Plum.	Ameixa.	ă-may′-ee-shă.
Pork; sucking-pig.	Porco; leitão.	pohr′-koo; lay-ee-tow^{n}′.
Port-wine.	Vinho do Porto.	veen′-yoo doo pohr′-too.
Potatoes, boiled, fried.	Batatas, cozidas, fritas.	bă-tah′-tăsh, koo-zee′-dăsh, free′-tăsh.
Potatoes, mashed, chipped.	Puré de batata, batatas fritas.	poo-re′ dĕ bă-tah′-tă, bă-tah′-tash free′-tăsh.
Prunes.	Ameixas secas.	ă-may′-ee-shăsh say′-kăsh.

English	Portuguese	Pronunciation
Pudding.	O pudim.	oo poo-dee^{n}′.
Rabbit.	Coelho.	koo-ayl′-yoo.
Radishes.	Rabanetes.	ră-bă-naytsh′.
Raspberries.	Framboesas.	fra^{n}-bwe′-zăsh.
Rice.	O arroz.	oo ă-rosh′.
Roasted.	Assado.	ă-sah′-doo.
Roll.	Pãozinho.	pow^{n}-zeen′-yoo.
Salad.	Salada	să-lah′-dă.
Salt.	O sal.	oo sal.
Salmon.	O salmão.	oo sal-mow^{n}′.
Sandwich.	Uma sanduíche.	oo′-mă sa^{n}d-weesh′.
Sardines.	Sardinhas.	săr-deen′-yăsh.
Sauce.	Molho.	mohl′-yoo.
Saucer.	Um pires.	oo^{n} pee′-rĕsh.
Sausage.	Salsicha, chouriço.	sal-see′-shă, shoh-ree′-soo.
Shell-fish.	Mariscos.	mă-reesh′-koosh.
Sherry.	Vinho de Xerez.	veen′-yoo dĕ shĕ-resh′.

Shrimps. | Camarões.
kă-mă-roy^{n}sh′.

Snacks, titbits. | Petiscos.
pĕ-teesh′-koosh.

Sole. | Linguado.
lee^{n}-gwah′-doo.

Soup. | Sopa.
soh′-pă.

Spinach. | O espinafre.
oo ish-peen-afr′.

Spoon. | Uma colher.
oo′-mă kool-yair′.

Squid. | Lula.
loo′-lă.

Stew. | Guisado.
gee-zah′-doo.

Strawberries. | Morangos.
moo-ra^{n}′-goosh.

Sugar. | O açúcar.
oo ă-soo′-kăr.

Syrup, fruit-essence. | O xarope.
oo shă-rop′.

Table, table-cloth. | Mesa, toalha de mesa.
may′-ză, too-al′-yă dĕ may′-ză.

Tea, tea-pot. | O chá, o bule.
oo shah, oo bool.

Toast. | Torradas.
too-rah′-dăsh.

Tomato. | O tomate.
oo too-maht′.

Tongue. | Língua.
lee^{n}′-gwă.

Toothpick. | Palito.
pă-lee′-too.

Tray. | Bandeja, taboleiro.
ba^{n}-day′-zhă, tă-boo-lay′-ee-roo.

Tunny. | O atum.
oo ă-too^{n}′.

Turkey. | O perú.
oo pĕ-roo′.

Veal. | Carne de vitela.
karn dĕ vee-te′-lă.

Vegetables. | Os legumes.
oozh lĕ-goomsh′.

Vegetarian diet. | O regime vegetariano.
oo re-zheem′ vĕ-zhĕ-tă-ree-ă′-noo.

Vinegar. | O vinagre.
oo vee-nagr′.

Water. | Água.
ag′-wă.

Whisky, and soda. | O whisky, com soda.
oo "whisky", ko^{n} so′-dă.

Wine, red, white. | Vinho, tinto, branco.
veen′-yoo, tee^{n}′-too, bra^{n}′-koo.

Wine, sweet, medium-sweet, medium-dry, dry. | Vinho, doce, meio-doce, meio-seco, seco.
veen′-yoo, dohs, may′-yoo dohs, may′-yoo say′-koo, say′-koo.

ENTERTAINMENT

Cinema performances are usually from 3 p.m. to 6 p.m., 6 p.m. to 9 p.m., 9 p.m. to midnight; theatre shows from 9.30 p.m. to midnight. Seats are often booked in advance. Smoking is forbidden within the cinema or theatre. The "typical" restaurants where 'fados' can be heard remain open until 2 a.m. or later.

Where is the —— cinema?	Onde fica o cinema...?

o^{n}d fee′-kă oo see-nay′-mă...

Are there any good films on?	Há agora bons filmes?

ah ă-go′-ră bo^{n}sh feelmsh.

What time does the show start?	A que horas começa?

ă kee o′-răsh koo-me′-să.

When does the main film begin?	Quando começa o filme principal?

kwa^{n}′-doo koo-me′-să oo feelm pree^{n}-see-pal′.

When does it end?	Quando acaba?

kwa^{n}′-doo ă-kah′-bă.

Where is the booking office?	Onde fica a bilheteira?

o^{n}d fee′-kă ă beel-yĕ-tay′-ee-ră.

I want to book some seats for this afternoon, this evening, tomorrow.	Quero reservar uns lugares para esta tarde, esta noite, amanhã.

kair′-oo rĕ-zĕr-var′ oonzh loo-garsh′ pă′-ră esh′-tă tard, esh′-tă noh′-eet, a-măn-ya^{n}′.

I want two seats in the stalls, the balcony.	Quero dois lugares na plateia, no balcão.

kair′-oo doh′-eezh loo-garsh′ nă plă-te′-yă, noo bal-kow^{n}′.

Have you anything better, cheaper?	Tem lugares melhores, mais baratos?

te^{n} loo-garsh′ mĕl-yorsh′, mȳzh bă-rah′-toosh.

They are too near, too far back.	Estão muito perto, muito atrás.

ish-tow^{n}′ mwee^{n}′-too pair′-too, mwee^{n}′-too ă-trash′.

I want seats nearer the centre.	Quero lugares mais ao meio.

kair′-oo loo-garsh′ mȳz ow may′-yoo.

How much is it?	Quanto é?

kwa^{n}′-too e.

Give me a programme.	Dê-me um programa.

day′-mee oo^{n} proo-gră′-mă.

I can't find my seat.	Não encontro o meu lugar.

now^{n} e^{n}-ko^{n}′-troo oo may′-oo loo-gar′.

When is the interval?	Quando é o intervalo?

kwa^{n}′-doo e oo ee^{n}-tĕr-va′-loo.

How long does it last?	Quanto tempo dura?

kwa^{n}′-too te^{n}′-poo doo′-ră.

No smoking allowed.	É proibido fumar.

e proo-ee-bee′-doo foo-mar′.

Way out, way in.	Saída, entrada.

să-ee′-dă, e^{n}-trah′-dă.

Documentary film, news reel.	O documentário, o noticiário.

oo doo koo-me^{n}-tah′-ree-oo, oo noo-tee-see-ah′-ree-oo.

I should like to go to a dance.	Gostava de ir a um baile.

goosh-tah′-vă deer ă oo^{n} bȳl.

I should like to dance.	Gostava de dançar.

goosh-tah′-vă dĕ da^{n}-sar′.

I don't dance, well.	Não sei dançar, bem.

now^{n} say′-ee da^{n}-sar′, be^{n}.

Will you dance with me? | Quer dançar comigo?
kair da^{n}-sar′ koo-mee′-goo.

May I have the honour of this dance? | V. Exª dança?
vos-esh-sĕ-le^{n}′-see-ă da^{n}′-să.

Can you dance the ——? | Sabe dançar...?
sahb da^{n}-sar′...

Waltz, tango, samba. | A valsa, o tango, o samba.
ă val′-să, oo ta^{n}′-goo, oo sam′-bă.

The band is very good. | A orquestra é muito boa.
ă or-kesh′-tră e mwee^{n}′-too boh′-ă.

What is the name of this tune? | Como se chama esta música?
koh′-moo sĕ shă′-mă esh′-tă moo′-zee-kă.

Will you have some refreshments? | Quer tomar alguma coisa?
kair too-mar′ al-goo′-mă koh′-ee-ză.

Shall we dance again? | Vamos dançar outra vez?
vă′-moozh da^{n}-sar′ oh′-tră vaysh.

It is very hot in here. | Faz muito calor aqui.
fazh mwee^{n}′-too kă-lohr′ ă-kee′.

Would you like to sit down? | Deseja sentar-se?
dĕ-zay′-zhă se^{n}-tars′.

It is cooler outside. | Está mais fresco lá fora.
ish-ta′ mȳsh fresh′-koo lah fo′-ră.

May I see you home? | Posso acompanhá-la a casa?
po′-soo ă-ko^{n}-păn-ya′-lă ă kah′-ză.

May I see you again? | Posso encontrá-la outra vez?
po′-soo e^{n}-ko^{n}-tra′-lă oh′-tră vaysh.

Actor, actress. | O actor, a actriz.
oo a-tohr′, ă at-reesh′.

English	Portuguese	Pronunciation
Choir.	Coro.	koh′-roo.
Concert.	Concerto.	ko^{n}-sayr′-too.
Folk-dancing group.	O rancho popular.	oo ra^{n}′-shoo poo-poo-lar′.
Two performances a day.	Dois espectáculos por dia.	doh′-eez ish-pe-ta′-koo-loosh poor dee′-ă.
Play.	Comédia, drama, peça.	koo-me′-dee-ă, dră′-mă, pe′-să.
Revue.	Revista.	rĕ-veesh′-tă.
Screen; stage.	Tela, écran; palco.	tay′-lă, ek-ra^{n}′; pal′-koo.
Night club.	Um clube nocturno.	oo^{n} kloob no-toor′-noo.
"Typical" restaurant.	Um restaurante típico.	oo^{n} rĕsh-tow-ra^{n}t′ tee′-pee-koo.
Bull-ring.	A praça de touros.	ă prah′-să dĕ toh′-roosh.
Bull-fighter.	Toureiro.	toh-ray′-ee-roo.
I should like to see a bull-fight.	Desejava ver uma corrida de touros.	dĕ-zĕ-zhah′-vă vayr oo′-mă koo-ree′-dă dĕ toh′-roosh.
Is there a good fight on?	A corrida é boa?	ă koo-ree′-dă e boh′-ă.
I want a seat in the shade, in the sun.	Quero um lugar à sombra, ao sol.	kair′-oo oo^{n} loo-gar′ ah so^{n}′-bră, ow sol.
I want a seat in the first row, second row.	Quero um lugar na barreira, na contra-barreira	air′-oo oo^{n} loo-gar′ nă bă-ray′-ee-ră, nă ko^{n}-tră-bă-ray′-ee-ră.

RADIO

Is there a wireless here? | Há cá um rádio?

ah ka oo^{n} rah′-dee-oo.

Can you get London? | Pode apanhar Londres?

pod ă-păn-yar′ lo^{n}′-drĕsh.

I wanted to hear the news. | Queria ouvir o noticiário.

kĕ-ree′-ă oh-veer′ oo noo-tee-see-ah′-ree-oo.

I want to hear some music | Quero ouvir música.

kair′-oo oh-veer′ moo′-zee-kă.

The wireless is making a lot of noise. | O rádio faz muito ruído.

oo rah′-dee-oo fazh mwee^{n}-too roo-ee′-doo.

It disturbs me, at night. | Incomoda-me, à noite.

ee^{n}-koo-mo′-dă-mĕ, ah noh′-eet.

Can you turn it down? | Pode baixá-lo?

pod bȳ-sha′-loo.

Please turn it off. | Faz favor de fechá-lo.

fash fă-vohr′ dĕ fĕ-sha′-loo.

It is a nuisance. | É muito incómodo.

e mwee^{n}′-too ee^{n}-ko′-moo-doo.

How do you work this set? | Como se põe a trabalhar este aparelho?

koh′-moo sĕ poy^{n} ă tră-băl-yar′ aysht ă-pă-rayl′-yoo.

Long-wave, medium-wave, short-wave. | Ondas compridas, médias, curtas.

o^{n}′-dăsh ko^{n}-pree′-dăsh, me′-dee-ăsh, koor′-tăsh.

SPORT

Are you interested in sport? | Os desportos interessam-lhe?

oozh dish-por′-toosh ee^{n}-tĕ-re′-sow^{n}-lyĕ.

I like watching games. | Gosto de ir ver jogar.

gohsh′-too deer vayr zhoo-gar′.

What games do you play? | Que desportos pratica?

kĕ dish-por′-toosh pră-tee′-kă.

I don't play any games. | Não pratico nenhum desporto.

now^{n} pră-tee′-koo nĕn-yoo^{n}′ dish-pohr′-too.

I play tennis, golf. | Jogo o ténis, o golfe.

zhoh′-goo oo te′-neesh, oo golf.

Is there a tennis court near here? | Há um campo (court) de ténis perto daqui?

ah oo^{n} ka^{n}′-poo (kohrt) dĕ te′-neesh pair′-too dă-kee′.

Is there a golf course here? | Há cá um campo de golfe?

ah ka oo^{n} ka^{n}′-poo dĕ golf.

I need a tennis racket. | Preciso de uma raqueta.

prĕ-see′-zoo doo′-mă ră-kay′-tă.

I need golf clubs. | Preciso de uns estiques de golfe.

prĕ-see′-zoo doonz ish-teekzh′ dĕ golf.

Tennis-balls, golf-balls. | Bolas de ténis, de golfe.

bo′-lăzh dĕ te′-neesh, dĕ golf.

What is your handicap? | Quanto dá de partido?

kwa^{n}′-too da dĕ păr-tee′-doo.

I should like to see a football match. | Gostava de ver um desafio de futebol.

goosh-tah′-vă dĕ vayr oo^{n} dĕ-ză-fee′-oo dĕ foot′-bol.

How does one get to the ground? | Como se vai para o campo?

koh′-moo sĕ vȳ pă′-ră oo ka^{n}′-poo.

Two tickets for the stand. | Duas bancadas.

doo′-ăzh ba^{n}-kah′-dăsh.

Who won? | Quem ganhou?

ke^{n} găn-yoh′.

The result was 4-1, 2-0. | O resultado foi quatro a um, dois a zero.

o rĕ-zool-tah′-doo foh′-ee kwat′-roo ă oo^{n}, doh′-eez ă zair′-oo.

A draw. | Um empate.
oo^{n} e^{n}-pat′.

The horse-race. | A corrida (de cavalos).
ă koo-ree′-dă dĕ kă-va′-loosh.

Bet, to bet. | Uma aposta, apostar.
oom ă-posh′-tă, ă-poosh-tar′.

Bicycle, cyclist. | Bicicleta, um ciclista.
bee-see-kle′-tă, oo^{n} see-kleesh′-tă.

Player. | Jogador.
zhoo-gă-dohr′.

I should like to go riding. | Queria montar a cavalo.
kĕ-ree′-ă mo^{n}-tar′ ă kă-va′-loo.

I should like to go for a swim. | Queria nadar.
kĕ-ree′-ă nă-dar′.

I should like to go sailing. | Queria ir num barco à vela.
kĕ-ree′-ă eer noo^{n} bar′-koo ah ve′-lă.

Can I hire a boat? | Posso alugar um barco?
po′-soo ă-loo-gar′ oo^{n} bar′-koo.

Bathing-tent, awning. | Barraca, toldo.
bă-rah′-kă, tohl′-doo.

Beach-guard, attendant. | Banheiro.
băn-yay′-ee-roo.

Beach police. | Cabo-de-mar.
kah′-boo dĕ mar.

Deep, (shallow), water. | Água funda (pouco funda).
ag′-wă foo^{n}′-dă (poh′-koo foo^{n}′-dă).

Is it safe, dangerous? | É seguro, perigoso?
e sĕ-goo′-roo, pĕ-ree-goh′-zoo.

Current. | A corrente.
ă koo-re^{n}t′.

Are my things safe here? | As minhas coisas estão seguras aqui?
ăzh meen′-yăsh koh′-ee-zăz ish-tow^{n}′ sĕ-goo′-răz ă-kee′.

Shooting, fishing.	Caçar (de espingarda), pescar.

kă-sar′ (dish-peeⁿ-gar′-dă), pĕsh-kar′.

Do I need a licence?	Preciso de uma licença?

prĕ-see′-zoo doo′-mă lee-seⁿ′-să.

Where do I get a licence?	Onde posso obter uma licença?

oⁿd po′-soo ob-tayr′ oo′-mă lee-seⁿ′-să.

Big game hunting.	Caça grossa.

kah′-să gro′-să.

Camp, to camp.	Acampamento, acampar.

ă-kaⁿ-pă-meⁿ′-too, ă-kaⁿ-par′.

Cartridges.	Cartuchos.

kăr-too′-shoosh.

To check equipment.	Verificar o equipamento.

vĕ-ree-fee-kar′ oo e-kee-pă-meⁿ′-too.

Danger.	Perigo.

pĕ-ree′-goo.

Guide.	O guia.

oo gee′-ă.

To halt.	Parar.

pă-rar′.

Hut.	Cabana, palhoça.

kă-bă′-nă, păl-yo′-să.

Knife.	Faca.

fah′-kă.

Lamp.	Lâmpada.

laⁿ′-pă-dă.

Map.	O mapa.

oo ma′-pă.

Net.	A rêde.

ă rayd.

Porter, bearer.	Carregador.

kă-rĕ-gă-dohr′.

Prohibited.	Proibido.
	proo-ee-bee′-doo.
Reserve.	Reserva.
	rĕ-zair′-vă.
Rifle.	Espingarda, carabina.
	ish-pee^{n}-gar′-dă, kă-ră-bee′-nă.
Rope.	Corda.
	kor′-dă.
Stove.	O fogão.
	oo foo-gow^{n}′.
Tent.	Tenda.
	te^{n}′-dă.
Torch.	Lâmpada eléctrica.
	la^{n}′-pă-dă ee-le′-tree-kă.
Track.	Pista.
	peesh′-tă.

MOTORING

Car. | O automóvel.
oo ow-too-mo'-věl.

Garage. | A garagem.
ă gă-rah'-zhe^{n}.

Petrol pump. | Bomba de gasolina.
bo^{n}'-bă dĕ gă-zoo-lee'-nă.

Petrol station. | A estação de serviço.
ă ish-tă-sow^{n}' dĕ sĕr-vee'-soo.

Repairs. | As reparações.
ăzh rĕ-pă-ră-soy^{n}sh'.

I want some petrol, water, oil. | Quero gasolina, água, óleo.
kair'-oo gă-zoo-lee'-nă, ag'-wă, o'-lee-oo.

Give me —— litres. | Dê-me...litros.
day'-mĕ...lee'-troosh.

Do I need oil as well? | Preciso de óleo também?
prĕ-see'-zoo do'-lee-oo tow^{n}-be^{n}'.

That will do. | Basta.
bash'-tă.

I need air in the tyres. | Os pneus precisam de ar.
oosh pnay'-oosh prĕ-see'-zow^{n} dar.

The tyres are a bit flat. | Os pneus estão um pouco vazios.
oosh pnay'-ooz ish-tow^{n}' oo^{n} poh'-koo vă-zee'-oosh.

Puncture. | Furo.
foo'-roo.

I don't know what is wrong. | Não sei o que tem.
now^{n} say'-ee oo kĕ te^{n}.

The trouble is here. | A avaria está aqui.
ă a-vă-ree'-ă ish-ta' ă-kee'.

This does not work. | Isto não funciona.
eesh′-too now^{n} foo^{n}-see-oh′-nă.

The engine will not start. | O motor não pega.
oo moo-tohr′ now^{n} pe′-gă.

The batteries are down. | As baterias precisam de ser carregadas.
ăzh bă-tĕ-ree′-ăsh prĕ-see′-zow^{n} dĕ sayr kă-rĕ-gah′-dăsh.

The lights won't work. | Os faróis não funcionam.
oosh fă-roysh′ now^{n} foo^{n}-see-oh′-now^{n}.

The engine, steering, starter. | O motor, a direcção, o motor de arranque.
oo moo-tohr′, ă dee-re-sow^{n}′, oo moo-tohr′ dă-ra^{n}k′.

The wheels, brakes. | As rodas, os travões.
ăzh ro′-dăsh, oosh tră-voy^{n}sh′.

Can you repair it? | Pode repará-lo?
pod rĕ-pă-ra′-loo.

Can I leave it here? | Posso deixá-lo aqui?
po′-soo day-ee-sha′-loo ă-kee′.

When will it be ready? | Quando estará pronto?
kwa^{n}′-doo ish-tă-ra′ pro^{n}′-too.

How much will it cost? | Quanto custará?
kwa^{n}′-too koosh-tă-ra′.

An overhaul of the car. | Uma vistoria geral do automóvel.
oo′-mă veesh-too-ree′-ă zhĕ-ral′ doo ow-too-mo′-vĕl.

To clean, wash. | Limpar, lavar.
lee^{n}-par′, lă-var′.

Can you give me a tow? | Pode rebocar-me?
pod rĕ-boo-kar′-mĕ.

Can you give me a lift? | Pode dar-me uma boleia?
pod dar′-mee oo′-mă boo-le′-yă.

How far is it to ——? | Qual é a distância até...?
kwal e ă deesh-ta^{n}′-see-ă ă-te′...

Can you show me the way on this map? — Pode mostrar-me o caminho neste mapa?

pod moosh-trar′-mee oo kă-meen′-yoo naysht ma′-pă.

Is there a car-ferry? — Há transporte de carros?

ah tra^{n}sh-port′ dĕ ka′-roosh.

Ferry-boat. — O "ferry-boat".

oo "ferry-boat".

You have to make for the bridge at —— — Tem de passar à ponte em...

te^{n} dĕ pă-sar′ ah po^{n}t e^{n}...

Accelerator, brake. — O acelerador, o travão.

oo ă-sĕ-lĕ-ră-dohr′, oo tră-vow^{n}′.

Battery, carburettor. — Bateria, o carburador.

bă-tĕ-ree′-ă, oo kăr-boo-ră-dohr′.

Clutch. — A embreagem.

ă e^{n}-bree-ah′-zhe^{n}.

Gear, first, second, third. — Primeira, segunda, terceira, velocidade.

preĕ-may′-ee-ră, sĕ-goo^{n}′-dă, tĕr-say′-ee-ră, vĕ-loo-see-dahd′.

Neutral. — Ponto morto.

po^{n}′-too mohr′-too.

Reverse gear. — A marcha-atrás.

ă mar-shă-trash′.

Direction-indicator. — Seta de direcção.

se′-ta dĕ dee-re-sow^{n}′.

Horn. — Buzina.

boo-zee′-nă.

Motor-cycle, lorry, scooter. — Motocicleta, o camião, o scooter.

moh-toh-see-kle′-tă, oo kă-mee-ow^{n}′, oo "scooter".

Number plate. — Chapa de matrícula.

sha′-pă dĕ mă-tree′-koo-lă.

Radiator. — O radiador.

oo ră-dee-ă-dohr′.

Sparking-plug. | Vela.
ve′-lă.

Speedometer. | O conta-quilómetros.
oo ko^{n}-tă-kee-lo′-mĕ-troosh.

Spring. | Mola.
mo′-lă.

Windscreen, windscreen-wiper. | O parabrisas, o limpa-parabrisas.
oo pă-ră-bree′-zăsh, oo lee^{n}′-pă pă-ră-bree′-zăsh.

There has been an accident. | Houve um desastre.
ohv oo^{n} dĕ-zashtr′.

We need a doctor, ambulance. | Precisamos de um médico, de uma ambulância.
prĕ-see-ză′-moosh doo^{n} me′-dee-koo, doom a^{n}-boo-la^{n}′-see-ă.

The car skidded. | O carro derrapou.
oo ka′-roo dĕ-ră-poh′.

It is (not) my fault. | A culpa (não) é minha.
ă kool′-pă (now^{n}) e meen′-yă.

I did not see (understand) the sign, signal. | Não vi (percebi) o sinal.
now^{n} vee (pĕr-sĕ-bee′) oo see-nal′.

I am a foreigner. | Sou estrangeiro.
soh ish-tra^{n}-zhay′-ee-roo.

Here is my driving-licence, passport. | Aqui está a minha carta de condução, o meu passaporte.
ă-kee′ ish-ta′ ă meen′-yă kar′-tă dĕ ko^{n}-doo-sow^{n}′, oo may′-oo pa-să-port′.

I am not used to driving here yet. | Ainda não estou acostumado a guiar aqui.
ă-ee^{n}′-da now^{n} ish-toh′ ă-koosh-too-mah′-doo ă gee-ar′ ă-kee′.

I forgot to keep to the right.	Esqueci-me de seguir pela direita.

ish-ke-see′-mĕ dĕ sĕ-geer′ pĕ′-lă dee-ray′-ee-tă.

He was driving too fast.	Ia com grande velocidade.

ee′-ă ko^{n} gra^{n}d vĕ-loo-see-dahd′.

He overtook me on the bend.	Ultrapassou-me na curva.

ool-tră-pă-soh′-mĕ nă koor′-vă.

He was on the wrong side of the road.	Ia no lado contrário do trânsito.

ee′-ă noo lah′-doo ko^{n}-trah′-ree-oo doo tra^{n}′-zee-too.

ROAD SIGNS

Curva perigosa.	Dangerous bend.

koor′-vă pĕ-ree-go′-ză.

Descida íngreme.	Steep hill.

dĕsh-see′-dă ee^{n}′-grĕm.

Desvio.	Diversion, detour.

dĕzh-vee′-oo.

Encruzilhada.	Crossroads.

e^{n}-kroo-zeel-yah′-dă.

Estacionamento proibido.	No parking.

ish-ta-see-oo-nă-me^{n}′-too proo-ee-bee′-doo.

Estrada sem continuação.	No through road.

ish-trah′-dă se^{n} ko^{n}-tee-noo-ă-sow^{n}′.

Guiar com cuidado.	Drive with care.

gee-ar′ ko^{n} kwee-dah′-doo.

Parar.	Stop.

pă-rar′.

Passagem de nível.	Level crossing.

pă-sah′-zhe^{n} dĕ nee′-vĕl.

Perigo. | Danger.
pě-ree′-goo.

Posto de socorros. | First-aid post.
pohsh′-too dě soo-koh′-roosh.

Proibido entrar. | No entrance.
proo-ee-bee′-doo e^{n}-trar′.

Seguir pela direita, esquerda. | Keep right, left.
sě-geer′ pě′-lă dee-ray′-ee-tă, ish-kayr′-dă.

Sentido único. | One-way street.
se^{n}-tee′-doo oo′-nee-koo.

Trabalhos. | Road up; repairs.
tră-bal′-yoosh.

Trânsito vedado. | Road closed.
tra^{n}′-zee-too vě-dah′-doo.

Velocidade máxima. | Maximum speed.
vě-loo-see-dahd′ ma′-see-mă.

COUNTRIES, NATIONALITIES AND PLACES

The Portuguese usually use 'England' and 'the English' as equivalents of 'Britain' and 'the British'. 'Americano' is nowadays the normal term for a citizen of the U.S.A. (Appended is the pronunciation of some place names.)

America, American. | América, americano.
ă-me'-ree-kă, ă-mĕ-ree-kă'-noo.

Angola. | Angola.
a^{n}-go'-lă.

Azores. | Os Açores.
ooz ă-soh'-rĕsh.

Brazil, Brazilian. | O Brasil, brasileiro.
o bră-zeel', bră-zee-lay'-ee-roo.

British. | Britânico.
bree-tă'-nee-koo.

Canada, Canadian. | O Canadá, canadiano.
oo kă-nă-da', kă-nă-dee-ă'-noo.

Cape Verde. | Cabo Verde.
kah'-bo verd.

England, English. | Inglaterra, inglês.
ee^{n}-glă-te'-ră, ee^{n}-glaysh'.

Great Britain. | Grã-Bretanha.
gra^{n} brĕ-tăn'-yă.

Ireland, Irish. | Irlanda, irlandês.
eer-la^{n}'-dă, eer-la^{n}-daysh'.

Madeira. | Madeira.
mă-day'-ee-ră.

Mozambique. | Moçambique.
moo-sow^{n}-beek'.

Portugal, Portuguese. | Portugal, português.
poor-too-gal', poor-too-gaysh'.

Rhodesia, Rhodesian. | A Rodésia, rodesiano.
ă roo-de'-zee-ă, roo-dĕ-zee-ă'-noo.

Scotland, Scottish. | Escócia, escocês.
ish-ko'-see-ă, ish-koo-saysh'.

South Africa, South African. | A África do Sul, sul-africano.
a'-free-kă do sool, sool-ă-free-kă'-noo.

Spain, Spanish. | Espanha, espanhol.
ish-păn'-yă, ish-păn-yol'.

U.S.A. | Os Estados Unidos.
ooz ish-tah'-dooz oo-nee'-doosh.

Wales, Welsh. | O País de Gales, galês.
oo pă-eezh' dĕ galsh, gă-lavsh'.

Alcobaça.
al-koo-bah'-să.

Aveiro.
ă-vay'-ee-roo.

Batalha.
bă-tal'-yă.

Buçaco. (Bussaco.)
boo-sah'-koo.

Cascais.
kash-kȳsh'.

Coimbra.
koo-ee^{n}'-bră.

Covilhã.
koo-veel-ya^{n}'.

(O) Douro (river).
oo doh'-roo.

Estoril.
ish-too-reel'.

Évora.
e′-voo-ră.

Figueira do Foz.
fee-gay′-ee-ră dă fosh.

Funchal.
foo^{n}-shal′.

Guimarães.
gee-mă-rȳ^{n}sh′.

Leixões.
lay-ee-shoy^{n}sh′.

Lisboa. (Lisbon.)
leezh-boh′-ă.

(O) Porto. (Oporto.)
(oo) pohr′-too.

Praia da Rocha.
prȳ′-yă dă ro′-shă.

Santarém.
sa^{n}-tă-re^{n}′.

Sintra. (Cintra.)
see^{n}′-tră.

(O) Tejo. (The Tagus.)
(oo) tay′-zhoo.

NUMERALS

0 Zero.
zair′-oo.

1 Um.
oo^{n}.

2 Dois.
doh′-eesh.

3 Três.
traysh.

4 Quatro.
kwat′-roo.

5 Cinco.
see^{n}′-koo.

6 Seis.
say′-eesh.

7 Sete.
set.

8 Oito.
oh′-ee-too.

9 Nove.
nov.

10 Dez.
desh.

11 Onze.
o^{n}z.

12 Doze.
dohz.

13 Treze.
trayz.

14 Catorze.
kă-tohrz′.

15 Quinze.
kee^{n}z.

16 Dezasseis.
dě-ză-say′-eesh.

17 Dezassete.
dě-ză-set′.

18 Dezoito.
de-zoh′-ee-too.

19 Dezanove.
dě-ză-nov′.

20 Vinte.
vee^{n}t.

21 Vinte-e-um.
vee^{n}t-ee-oo^{n}′.

22 Vinte-e-dois.
vee^{n}t-ee-doh′-eesh.

30 Trinta.
tree^{n}′-tă.

40 Quarenta.
kwă-re^{n}′-tă.

50 Cinquenta.
see^{n}-kwe^{n}′-tă.

60 Sessenta.
sě-se^{n}′-tă.

70 Setenta.
sě-te^{n}′-tă.

80 Oitenta.
oh-ee-te^{n}′-tă.

90 Noventa.
noo-ve^{n}′-tă.

100 Cento; cem (before noun).
se^{n}'-too; se^{n}.

101 Cento-e-um.
se^{n}'-too ee oo^{n}.

200 Duzentos.
doo-ze^{n}'-toosh.

300 Trezentos.
trĕ-ze^{n}'-toosh.

400 Quatrocentos.
kwat-roo-se^{n}'-toosh.

500 Quinhentos.
keen-ye^{n}'-toosh.

600 Seiscentos.
say-eesh-se^{n}'-toosh.

700 Setecentos
set-se^{n}'-toosh.

800 Oitocentos.
oh-ee-too-se^{n}'-toosh.

900 Novecentos.
nov-se^{n}'-toosh.

1000 Mil.
meel.

2000 Dois mil.
doh'-eezh meel.

A million. Um milhão.
oo^{n} meel-yow^{n}'.

First, second.	Primeiro, segundo.
prĕ-may'-ee-roo, sĕ-goo^{n}'-doo.	
Third, fourth.	Terceiro, quarto.
tĕr-say'-ee-roo, kwar'-too.	
Fifth, sixth.	Quinto, sexto.
kee^{n}'-too, sesh'-too.	
Half, a third.	A metade, a terça parte.
ă mee-tahd', ă tayr'-să part.	
A quarter, two thirds.	A quarta parte, dois terços.
ă kwar'-tă part, doh'-eesh tayr'-soosh.	

(*Note:* "*Três*" (3) *and* "*Treze*" (13) *may be confused when they stand immediately before a vowel* (*e.g. três escudos; treze escudos*). "*Treze*" *is, therefore, often pronounced* "*tray'-zee*" *for the sake of clarity.*)

TIME

DAYS OF THE WEEK

Sunday. | Domingo.
doo-mee^{n}′-goo.

Monday, Tuesday. | Segunda-feira, têrça-feira.
sĕ-goo^{n}′-dă fay′-ee-ră, tayr′-să fay′-ee-ră.

Wednesday, Thursday. | Quarta-feira, quinta-feira.
kwar′-tă fay′-ee-ră, kee^{n}′-tă fay′-ee-ră.

Friday. | Sexta-feira.
sesh-tă fay′-ee-ră.

Saturday. | Sábado.
sa′-bă-doo.

(*Note: In railway time-tables and public announcements the days from Monday to Friday are often abbreviated thus:*

às 2as *(or, às segundas): on Mondays.*
às 6as *(or, às sextas): on Fridays.*)

MONTHS

January, February. | Janeiro, fevereiro.
zhă-nay′-ee-roo, fĕv-ray′-ee-roo.

March, April. | Março, abril.
mar′-soo, ă-breel′.

May, June. | Maio, junho.
mȳ′-oo, zhoon′-yoo.

July, August. | Julho, agosto.
zhool′-yoo, ă-gohsh′-too.

September, October. — Setembro, outubro.
sĕ-te^{n}′-broo, oh-too′-broo.

November, December. — Novembro, dezembro.
noo-ve^{n}′-broo, dĕ-ze^{n}′-broo.

(*Note: Dates can be expressed thus:*
May 1st: O primeiro de maio.
June 2nd: O dia dois de junho.
August 23rd: O dia vinte-e-três de agosto.
On April 3rd: No dia três de abril.
On March 1st: No primeiro de março.)

SEASONS AND HOLIDAYS

Season (of the year). — A estação (do ano).
ă ish-tă-sow^{n}′ (doo ă′-noo).

A holiday. — Um dia feriado.
oo^{n} dee′-ă fĕ-ree-ah′-doo.

Holidays. — Férias.
fe′-ree-ăsh.

Christmas. — O Natal.
oo nă-tal′.

Easter. — A Páscoa.
ă pash′-kwă.

Spring, summer. — A primavera, o verão.
ă pree-mă-vair′-ă, oo vĕ-row^{n}′.

Autumn, winter. — O outono, o inverno.
oo oh-toh′-noo, oo ee^{n}-vair′-noo.

GENERAL TIME PHRASES

Day, week. — Um dia, uma semana.
oo^{n} dee′-ă, oo′-mă sĕ-mă′-nă.

Fortnight. — Quinze dias.
kee^{n}z dee′-ăsh.

Month. — Um mês.
oo^{n} maysh.

Three months.	Três meses.
trayzh may'-zĕsh.	
Year, two years.	Um ano, dois anos.
oo^{n} ă'-noo, doh'-eez ă'-noosh.	
Morning, afternoon (or evening), night.	A manhã, a tarde, a noite.
ă măn-ya^{n}', ă tard, ă noh'-eet.	
To-day, yesterday.	Hoje, ontem.
ohzh, o^{n}'-te^{n}.	
Day before yesterday.	Anteontem.
a^{n}-tee-o^{n}'-te^{n}.	
Yesterday evening (or afternoon), morning.	Ontem de tarde, pela manhã.
o^{n}'-te^{n} dĕ tard, pĕ'-lă măn-ya^{n}'.	
Tomorrow.	Amanhã.
a-măn-ya^{n}'.	
Tomorrow morning, afternoon.	Amanhã de manhã, de tarde.
a-măn-ya^{n}' dĕ măn-ya^{n}', dĕ tard.	
Day after tomorrow.	Depois de amanhã.
dĕ-poh'-eezh da-măn-ya^{n}'.	
Last week.	A semana passada.
ă sĕ-măn'-ă pă-sah'-dă.	
Last month, year.	O mês, ano, passado.
oo maysh, ă'-noo, pă-sah'-doo.	
A month, week, ago.	Há um mês, uma semana.
ah oo^{n} maysh, oo'-mă sĕ-mă'-nă.	
Every day, daily.	Todos os dias, diàriamente.
toh'-dooz oozh dee'-ăsh, dee-ah-ree-ă-me^{n}t'.	
I have been here since Sunday.	Estou cá desde domingo.
ish-toh' ka' dezh'-dĕ doo-mee^{n}'-goo.	

I have been here four days. | Há quatro dias que estou cá.

ah kwat′-roo dee′-ăsh kee ish-toh′ ka.

THE CLOCK

What time is it? | Que horas são?

kee o′-răsh sow^{n}.

It is one o'clock. | É uma hora.

e oo′-mă o′-ră.

It is ten o'clock. | São dez horas.

sow^{n} dez o′-răsh.

Quarter past two. | Duas e um quarto.

doo′-ăz ee oo^{n} kwar′-too.

Quarter to nine. | Quinze minutos para as nove.

kee^{n}z mĕ-noo′-toosh pă-razh′ nov.

It is 12 o'clock (midday). | É meio-dia.

e may′-yoo dee′-ă.

It is half-past twelve (in afternoon). | É meio-dia e meia-ora.

e may′-yoo dee′-ă ee may′-yă o′-ră.

It is 12 o'clock (midnight). | É meia-noite.

e may′-yă noh′-eet.

It is twenty past five. | São cinco e vinte.

sow^{n} see^{n}′-koo ee veent.

It is ten to three. | São dez minutos para as três.

sow^{n} dezh mĕ-noo′-toosh pă-rash′ traysh.

WEIGHTS AND MEASURES

The metric system is used in Portugal. The following tables give approximate equivalents:

WEIGHT

100 gramas	=	3½ oz.
1 quilograma	=	2 lb. 3 oz.

CAPACITY

1 litro	=	1¾ pints.
4½ litros	=	1 gallon.

LENGTH

1 centímetro	=	⅜ inch.
2½ centímetros	=	1 inch.
30 centímetros	=	1 foot.
91 centímetros	=	1 yard.
1 metro	=	39 inches.
1 quilómetro	=	0·62 mile.
1·6 quilómetros	=	1 mile.

TEMPERATURE

To convert degrees Centigrade into degrees Fahrenheit, multiply by $\frac{9}{5}$ *and add* 32. *Thus,* 20° *C.*=68° *F.* ($20 \times \frac{9}{5} + 32 = 68$).

SOME PUBLIC NOTICES

Aberto. | Open.
ă-bair′-too.

Agência de viagens. | Travel agency.
ă-zhe^{n}′-see-ă dĕ vee-ah′-zhe^{n}sh.

Água potável. | Drinking water.
ag′-wă poo-tah′-vĕl.

Alfândega. | Customs.
al-fa^{n}′-dĕ-gă.

Aluga-se. | For hire, to let.
ă-loo′-găs.

Apertar. | Press.
ă-pĕr-tar′.

Assinatura. | Signature.
ă-see-nă-too′-ră.

Autocarro. | Bus.
ow-too-ka′-roo.

Bater. | Knock.
bă-tayr′.

Bilheteira. | Booking-office.
beel-yĕ-tay′-ee-ră.

Bombeiros. | Fire Brigade.
bo^{n}-bay′-ee-roosh.

Consulado. | Consulate.
ko^{n}-soo-lah′-doo.

Conto. | 1,000 escudos.
ko^{n}′-too.

Correio. | Post Office.
koo-ray′-yoo.

Embaixada. | Embassy.
e^{n}-bȳ-shah′-dă.

Empurrar. | Push.
e^{n}-poo-rar′.

Encerrado. | Closed.
e^{n}-sĕ-rah′-doo.

Entrada livre. | Admission free.
e^{n}-trah′-dă leevr.

Endereço. | Address.
e^{n}-dĕ-ray′-so.

Fechado. | Closed.
fĕ-shah′-doo.

Frio. | Cold.
free′-oo.

Homens. | Gentlemen (lavatory).
o′-me^{n}sh.

Informações. | Enquiries.
ee^{n}-foor-mă-soy^{n}sh′.

Leilão. | Auction.
lay-ee-low^{n}′.

Livre. | Free, vacant.
leevr.

Lotação esgotada. | House full.
loo-tă-sow^{n}′ izh-goo-tah′-dă.

Morada. | Address, residence.
moo-rah′-dă.

Não se debruçar. | Do not lean out.
now^{n} sĕ dĕ-broo-sar′.

Nome. | Name.
nohm.

Pensão. | Boarding-house.
pe^{n}-sow^{n}′.

Pensão completa. | Full board.
pe^{n}-sow^{n}′ ko^{n}-ple′-tă.

Perigo. | Danger.
pĕ-ree′-goo.

Proibido. proo-ee-bee′-doo.	Forbidden.
Puxar. poo-shar′.	Pull.
Rápido. ra′-pee-doo.	Express.
Retrete. rĕ-trayt′.	Lavatory.
Saída. să-ee′-dă.	Exit.
Saldo. sal′-doo.	Sale.
Senhoras. sĕn-yohr′-ăsh.	Ladies (lavatory).
Tocar. too-kar′.	Ring.
Trabalhos. tră-bal′-yoosh.	Repairs (roads, bridges, etc.).
Veneno. vĕ-nay′-noo.	Poison.

PORTUGUESE ABBREVIATIONS

A.C.P.	Automóvel Clube de Portugal.	Portuguese Automobile Club.
Av.	Avenida.	Avenue.
C^{a}, C^{ia}.	Companhia.	Company.
C.P.	Caminhos de ferro da Companhia Portuguesa.	Portuguese State Railways.
D.	Dom, Dona.	Mr., Mrs., Miss, (with Christian names only).
De 2^{a}.	de segunda classe.	2nd class (hotels, boarding-houses).
D., D^{to}.	direito.	On the right (in addresses of flats).
End. Teleg.	endereço telegráfico.	Telegram address.
Esc.	escudo.	Escudo.
E., Esq.	esquerdo.	On the left (in addresses of flats).
H.P.	—	Horse-power.
Idem.	—	Ditto.
Kg.	quilograma.	Kilogram.
Km.	quilómetro.	Kilometre.
Lda.	limitada.	Ltd.
M.	metro.	Metre.
N^{a}. Sr^{a}.	Nossa Senhora.	Our Lady.
P.	praça.	Square.
P.I.D.E.	Polícia internacional e de defesa do estado.	Security Police.
R.	rua.	Street.

R/C.	rés-do-chão.	Ground floor.
S., Sto, Sta.	são, santa, santo.	Saint.
S.N.I.	Secretariado Nacional da Informação.	State Tourist Bureau.
Soc.	sociedade.	Society (commerce).
Sr., Sra.	senhor, senhora.	Mr., Mrs., Miss.
Sucrs.	sucessores.	Successors (commerce).
T.A.P.	Transportes Aéreos Portugueses.	Portuguese Airways.
1° (andar)	primeiro (andar).	First floor.
2° (andar)	segundo (andar).	Second floor.

VOCABULÁRIO

As palavras escritas com letras maiúsculas indicam os títulos das várias secções do livro.

Abóbora, marrow, 108
ABREVIATURAS, abbreviations, 141
Abrigo, shelter, 63
Abril, April, 133
Acampamento, camp, 120
Acelerador, accelerator, 124
Acepipes variados, hors d'œuvres, 107
Acetona, nail-varnish remover, 75
ACIDENTE, accident, 95
Actor, actor, 115
Actriz, actress, 115
Açúcar, sugar, 111
Adesivo, plaster; adhesive tape, 73, 75
Adeus, good-bye, 21, 68
Aeroporto, airport, 45, 55
África do Sul, South Africa, 129
Agência aérea, air travel agency, 44
Agência de navegação, shipping agents, 41
Agosto, August, 133
Água, water, 33, 43, 52, 77, 99
Água filtrada, drinking water, 33
Água potável, drinking water, 138
Agulha, needle, 85
Alface, lettuce, 107
ALFÂNDEGA, customs, 46
Alfinetes, pins, 85
Alfinetes de segurança, safety-pins, 85
Algodão, cotton, 83
Algodão em rama, cotton wool, 73
Alho, garlic, 102, 106
Almoço, lunch, 33, 51, 101
Almofada, pillow, 33, 43
Ambulância, ambulance, 95, 125
Amêijoas, cockles, 105
Ameixa, plum, 109
Ameixas secas, prunes, 109
Amêndoas, almonds, 103
América, America, 128
Americano, American, 69, 128
Amigo, friend, 66, 67
Ananás, pineapple, 109
Ano, year, 135
Anteontem, day before yesterday, 135
Antiséptico, antiseptic, 73
Aparelho, radio set, 117
Aparo, nib, 80
Aposta, bet, 119
Apresentação, introduction, 66
Ar, air, 122
Arenque, herring, 107
Armação, frame (of spectacles), 91
Arroz, rice, 110
Aspirina, aspirin, 73
Assinatura, signature, 138
Atacadores de sapatos, shoe laces, 84
Atenção! Look out! 25
Atum, tunny, 112
Autocarro, bus, 58, 59, 138
AUTOMÓVEL, motor-car, 122
Avaria, trouble (damage), 122
AVIÃO, aeroplane, 44
AVISOS E LETREIROS, Public notices 138
Azeite, olive-oil, 108
Azeitonas, olives, 108
Azulejos, glazed tiles, 87

Bacalhau, cod, 105
Bacia, basin, 43
Bagageiro, porter, 34, 37
BAGAGEM, luggage, 34
Baile, dance, 114
Balcão, balcony, 113
Banana, banana, 103

Bancada, ticket (for stand), 118
BANCO, bank, 81
Bandeja, tray, 112
Banheiro, beach-guard, 119
Banho, bath, 50, 52
Bar, bar, 42, 51
Barco, boat, ship, 44, 119
Barraca, bathing-tent, 119
Batatas, potatoes, 109
Bateria, battery, 123, 124
Baton, lipstick, 75, 84
Beliche, berth, 42
Bengala, stick, 87
Bicicleta, bicycle, 119
Bife, beef-steak, 104
Bilhete, ticket, 29, 31, 41, 42
Bilhete de ida, single ticket, 32
Bilhete de ida e volta, return ticket, 32
Bilhetes postais, postcards, 38, 70
Bilheteira, ticket-office, 31, 37, 113
Bisnaga, tube (of paste), 76
Blusa, blouse, 82
Boa noite, good night, 21, 52
Boa tarde, good afternoon, 21
Boião, jar (of face cream), 75
Bolacha, biscuit, 104
Bolas de golfe, golf balls, 118
Bolas de ténis, tennis balls, 118
Bolo, cake, 104
Bom dia, good morning, 21, 52
Bomba, petrol pump, 122
Bombeiros, fire brigade, 138
Boquilha, cigarette-holder, 70
Borbulhas, blisters, 74
Bordados, embroidery, 84
Borracha, rubber, 81, 90
Borrego, lamb, 107
Borrifo, spray, 78
Botão, button, 82
Botões de punho, cuff-links, 83
Botões de colarinho, studs, 86
Braço, arm, 99
Brasil, Brazil, 128
Brasileiro, Brazilian, 128
Brilhantina líquida, hair-oil, 75
Brilhantina sólida, hair-cream, 75
Brinquedos, toys, 86
Bule, teapot, 111
Buzina, horn (of car), 124
Cabana, hut, 120
CABELEIREIRO, hairdresser, 76
Cabelo, hair, 77, 78
Cabide, coat-hanger, 83
Cabine telefónica, telephone kiosk, 38
Cabo-de-mar, beach police, 119
Caça grossa, big-game hunting, 120
Cachecol, scarf, 85
Cachimbo, pipe, 70
Cadeira de lona, deck chair, 44
Café, café; coffee, 29, 33
Cais, dock, 42, 55
Caixa, post-box, 70; cashier, 82
Calças, trousers, 87
Caldo verde, cabbage soup, 104
Calos, corns, 74
Cama de baixo, lower berth (bed), 33
Cama de cima, upper berth, 33
Camarões, shrimps, 111
Camarote, cabin, 42
Câmbio, rate of exchange, 81
Câmbio, casas de-, money changers, 81
Camião, lorry, 124
Caminho, way, 31, 63, 124
Caminho de ferro, railway, 31
Camisa, shirt, 85
Camisa de dormir, nightdress, 85
Campainha, bell, 40, 51
Campo, sports field, 118
Campo de golfe, golf course, 118
Campo de ténis, tennis court, 118
Canadá, Canada, 128
Canadiano, Canadian, 128
Caneta, fountain-pen, 80
Canja, chicken soup, 105
Carabina, rifle, 121
Caranguejo, crab, 105
Carburador, carburettor, 124
Carne, meat, 108
Carne assada, roast beef, 104
Carne fria, cold meat, 105
Carneiro, mutton, 108
Carregador, bearer, porter, 120
Carro, car, 125
Carro de linhas, cotton reel, 83
Carruagem-cama, sleeping-car, 32
Carta, letter, 38, 52, 70, 71

Minuto, minute, 35
Mise-en-pli, set (hair), 77
Mola, spring, 125
Molho, gravy, 106; sauce, 110
Morada, address, 82
Morangos, strawberries, 111
Mostarda, mustard, 108
Motocicleta, motor-cycle, 124
Motor, engine (of car), 123
Motor de arranque, starter, 131
Motorista, driver, 59
Mulher, wife, 67
Município, town hall, 61
Muséu de arte, art gallery, 60
Muséu histórico, museum, 60
Música, tune, 115; music, 117

Não, no, 21
Nata, cream, 105
Natal, Christmas, 134
Navalha de barba, razor, 75, 77
Negócios, business, 47
Noite, night, 117, 135
Nome, name, 26, 66, 71
Nota, note, 81, 99
Noticiário, news, 117; news reel, 114
Nozes, nuts, 108
Número, number, 28, 31, 50
NÚMEROS, numerals, 131

Objecto, item of luggage, 36
Obrigado, thank you, 21, 64
Obturação, filling, 97
Óculos, spectacles, 90, 91
Óculos escuros, sun glasses, 76, 86
Óleo, oil, 122
Olhos, eyes, 37, 73
Omeleta, omelette, 109
Ondas compridas, long waves, 117
Ondas curtas, short waves, 117
Ontem, yesterday, 135
Orquestra, band, 115
Ostras, oysters, 109
Outono, autumn, 134
Ouvido, ear, 99
Ovo, egg, 105
Ovo cozido, boiled egg, 106
Ovo escalfado, poached egg, 106
Ovo estrelado, fried egg, 106

Pacote, parcel, 35, 36
PAÍSES, countries, 128
País de Gales, Wales, 129
Palco, stage, 116
Palhoça, hut, 120
Palito, toothpick, 111
Paninhos, sanitary towels, 76
Pano, face cloth, 74
Pão, bread, 104
Pãozinho, roll, 110
Papel, paper, 80
Papel de embrulhar, brown paper, 80
Papel de escrever, writing paper, 80
Parabrisas, windscreen, 125
Paragem, stop (bus, tram), 59
Paragem, última —, terminus, 59
Parede, wall, 101
Páscoa, Easter, 134
Passagem, passage, 41
Passagem de nível, level crossing, 126
Passaporte, passport, 44, 46, 82
Passeio, walk, 25
Pasta, brief-case, 35
Pato, duck, 105
Peça, play, 116
Pedra, flint, 70
Pedra-pomes, pumice stone, 75
Pegadeira, handle, 92
Peixe, fish, 106
Películas, films, 79, 92
Películas a cores, coloured films, 79
PENSÃO, boarding house, 49
Pensão completa, full board, 50
Pensos, lint, 73
Pente, comb, 74
Pepino, cucumber, 105
Pequeno almoço, breakfast, 33
Pera, pear, 109
Perdiz, partridge, 109
Perigo, danger, 120
Perna, leg, 99
Perú, turkey, 112
Pés, feet, 74
Pescada, hake, 106
Pescoço, neck, 77
PESOS E MEDIDAS, Weights and Measures, 137
Pêssego, peach, 109
Petiscos, snacks, 111

INDEX

The words printed in capitals refer to Sections, in which the subject is dealt with at length.

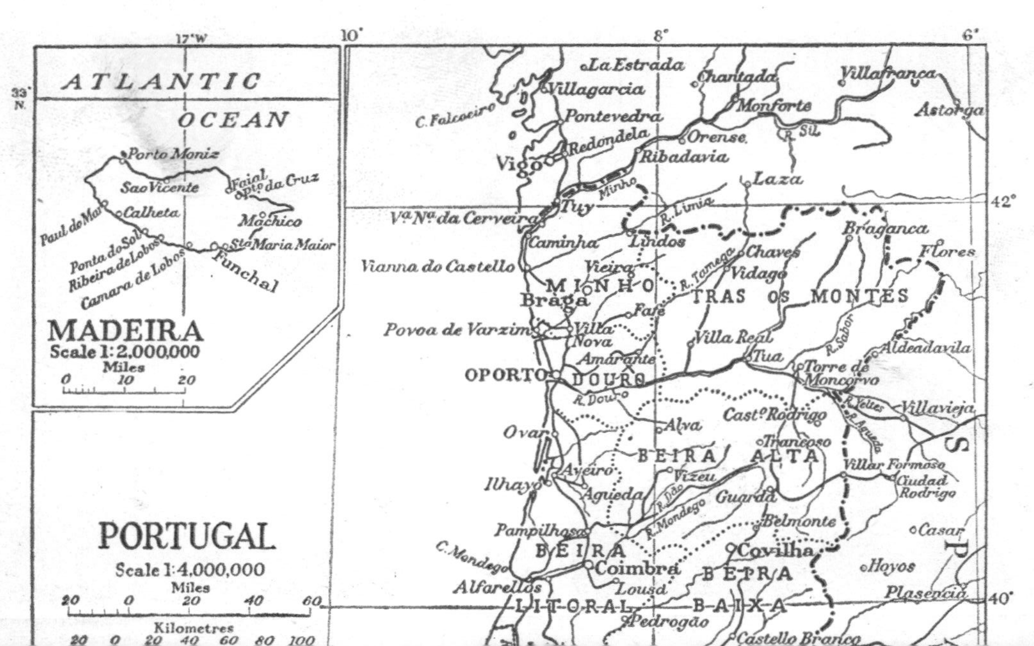
ATLANTIC
OCEAN
17°W
33° N.
Porto Moniz
Sao Vicente
Faial
Pto da Cruz
Calheta
Paul do Mar
Machico
Ponta do Sol
Ribeira de Lobos
Camara de Lobos
Sta Maria Maior
Funchal
MADEIRA
Scale 1:2,000,000
Miles
0 10 20
PORTUGAL
Scale 1:4,000,000
Miles
20 0 20 40 60
Kilometres
20 0 20 40 60 80 100
10°
8°
6°
42°
40°
La Estrada
Villagarcia
C. Falcoeiro
Pontevedra
Redondela
Vigo
Chantada
Monforte
Villafranca
Astorga
Orense
R. Sil
Ribadavia
Laza
Minho
Tuy
Va Na da Cerveira
R. Limia
Caminha
Lindos
Bragança
Flores
Chaves
Vianna do Castello
Vieira
R. Tamega
Vidago
MINHO
Braga
TRAS OS MONTES
Fafe
Povoa de Varzim
Villa Nova
Villa Real
R. Sabor
Aldeadavila
Amarante
Tua
Torre de Moncorvo
OPORTO
DOURO
R. Douro
R. Yeltes
Villavieja
Cast° Rodrigo
R. Agueda
Ovar
Alva
Trancoso
BEIRA ALTA
S
Aveiro
Vizeu
Villar Formoso
Ciudad Rodrigo
Ilhavo
Agueda
R. Dão
Guarda
R. Mondego
Belmonte
Pampilhosa
Casar
P
C. Mondego
BEIRA
Covilha
Hoyos
Coimbra
BEIRA
Alfarellos
Lousã
Plasencia
LITORAL
BAIXA
Pedrogão
Castello Branco